A Little Book of Perl

A Little Book on Perl

Robert W. Sebesta

University of Colorado
at Colorado Springs
Computer Science Department

Prentice Hall
Upper Saddle River, NJ 07458

Library of Congress Cataloging-in-Publication Data

Sebesta, Robert W.
    A little book on Perl / by Robert Sebesta.
       p. cm.
    ISBN 0-13-927955-5 (pbk.)
    1. Perl (Computer program language) I. Title

QA76.73.P22 S43 1999
005.13'3--dc21   99-051528
                                                     CIP

Publisher: *Tom Robbins*
Associate editor: *Alice Dworkin*
Production editor: *Audri Anna Bazlen*
Editor-in-chief: *Marcia Horton*
Executive managing editor: *Vince O'Brien*
Managing editor: *David A. George*
Vice-president of production and manufacturing: *David W. Riccardi*
Art director: *Jayne Conte*
Cover design: *Bruce Kenselaar*
Manufacturing buyer: *Pat Brown*
Marketing manager: *Danny Hoyt*

© 2000 by Prentice Hall
Prentice-Hall, Inc.
Upper Saddle River, New Jersey 07458

Author can be reached at: rws@cs.uccs.edu

The author and publisher of this book have used their best efforts in preparing this book. These efforts include the development, research, and testing of the theories and programs to determine their effectiveness. The author and publisher make no warranty of any kind, expressed or implied, with regard to these programs or the documentation contained in this book. The author and publisher shall not be liable in any event for incidental or consequential damages in connection with, or arising out of, the furnishing, performance, or use of these programs.

Printed in the United States of America
10 9 8 7 6 5 4 3 2 1

ISBN 0-13-927955-5

Prentice-Hall International (UK) Limited, *London*
Prentice-Hall of Australia Pty. Limited, *Sydney*
Prentice-Hall Canada Inc., *Toronto*
Prentice-Hall Hispanoamericana, S.A., *Mexico*
Prentice-Hall of India Private Limited, *New Delhi*
Prentice-Hall of Japan, Inc., *Tokyo*
Pearson Education Asia Pte Ltd
Editora Prentice-Hall do Brasil, Ltda., *Rio de Janeiro*

Dedicated to Larry Wall

Contents

Preface

This is a book on the widely used programming language, Perl. It includes both descriptions of the features of the language, and how they can be used to write useful programs. As is usually the case with books on programming, the examples are small and are designed to illustrate one or a few language capabilities. Larger, more complex programs often drown the features the book is trying to show, just by their size and structure.

The goal of the book is to provide a clear and concise description of Perl for someone who has programmed in some other programming language and wants to learn to use Perl. In many ways, Perl is similar to other programming languages; in some other ways, it is very different. We point out, whenever it is relevant, the advantages Perl offers over alternative languages.

Perl has been for some time the most widely used UNIX system administration language. It is now also the most popular scripting language for writing Common Gateway Interface (CGI) programs. In recent years, Perl has begun to replace C for many smaller programming tasks, especially if large files of text must be processed. Because of these varied applications of the language, there is now a large number of Perl users. Due to the dramatic rise inpopularity of the World Wide Web and, consequently, college courses that cover various aspects of it, including CGI programming, there is now an emerging academic market for Perl books. However, most, if not all, currently available books on Perl were written for the professional programmer. This book attempts to target experienced programmers, whether that experience has come from professional programming or in the first two courses in a degree program in computer science or a closely related field.

Perl is neither small nor simple. It is a complicated combination of the features and capabilities of previous languages, such as `sed`, `awk`, and C, along with a few new ideas of its own. Although Perl is powerful, it is relatively easy to learn enough of the language to write programs that describe significant processing, although the programs themselves are rather small.

This book is neither a comprehensive reference book nor a tutorial. Reference books about languages contain all of the details of the language, but usually in a form that is difficult to read. It is difficult to learn a programming language from such a book; it is like trying to learn English by studying a book on English grammar. On the other hand, tutorial books on programming languages often aim too low–they assume the reader knows little about programming languages and programming. Seasoned programmers, both professional and from collegiate experience, find such books boring and tedious, for they too often waste several paragraphs on the obvious.

Our intention is for this book to be between these two models. It will not cover every detail of Perl, nor will it provide an introduction to computers, programming, or programming languages. It is not for those who want to become Perl experts; they will still need a Perl reference book. On the other hand, it is not for those who want to learn just a bit about Perl to enable them to write (and read) a few relatively small and simple programs. Those people will want a brief tutorial that leaves out all of the advanced features.

Because the book is aimed at professional programmers and college students who have had at least two courses in programming, it gets to the point quickly, with little discussion of background topics such people should already know. The book will not assume that the reader knows awk or C, or even anything about UNIX. Of course, prior knowledge of awk or C will make learning Perl much easier. We have tried to make the book platform independent. Most Perl constructs work the same way on all platforms, including UNIX, Windows, and Macintosh. In those cases where there are differences, we point them out to the reader.

One of the unique features of this book is the sample program that appears in Chapter 1, before any details of Perl have been discussed. This is not a "hello world" program–it actually does something useful. It is followed by a brief line-by-line explanation of its statements. We hope this example will motivate the reader with both the power and brevity of Perl. It provides the reader with a quick look at a complete program, without first dragging him or her though a tedious discussion of the basics of Perl.

The book includes many code segments. Each of the 10 chapters has at least one complete program. The book does not contain descriptions of all of the Perl functions–these can be found on Web pages to which the book will refer. The book will not focus on UNIX system administration; rather, it will concentrate on Perl as a programming tool, which can be used for a variety of tasks. Because we believe that the number of PC Perl users is growing, we will not spend a great deal of time with UNIX-particular details at the expense of those PC users.

The programs and code segments in this book were developed and tested using Perl 5. Note that when we say "Perl," we mean the language and when we say "perl," we mean the Perl language-processing system (a compiler and an interpreter).

THE BOOK'S CONTENTS

The first chapter provides some overview of the purposes and origins of Perl. It also provides an introduction to what CGI programming is. Most importantly, it includes an example of a Perl program, including a brief description of each of its statements. Chapter 2 describes the small-scale features of Perl, covering enough constructs to allow small programs to be written. Chapter 3 describes most of the control statements. Chapter 4 covers Perl's arrays, which are more flexible and powerful than those of other popular programming languages. Chapter 5 describes hashes (which are data structures for storing keyed table information) and references (which provide some of the benefits of pointers without their inherent dangers). The anatomy of Perl's functions is the topic of Chapter 6, including some of the predefined functions. The powerful pattern-matching facilities of Perl are described in Chapter 7, which includes many small fragments of code that illustrate their power and flexibility. Files, file tests, and formats are described in Chapter 8. Chapter 9 provides the information required to write CGI programs in Perl, including the use of the convenient CGI.pm module. Included in Chapter 9 are several complete sample CGI programs. Finally, Chapter 10 has brief descriptions of six advanced topics of Perl that do not fit nicely into any of the previous chapters. Among these are how other programs can be launched from Perl programs, how a Perl program can communicate with other computers, and how graphical user interfaces can be added to Perl programs using Tk.

TO THE INSTRUCTOR

This book is meant to support a one- or two-semester credit course at the sophomore or junior level. The reader is expected to have had as a minimum an introductory course in programming and a course in data structures, or their equivalents in industrial experience. The book is also designed to be used as a supplement in courses on programming the World Wide Web.

For short courses, the last two chapters could be skipped. For longer courses, the last two chapters could be covered and perhaps given further attention through supplemental material on CGI and some of the advanced aspects of Perl.

TO THE PROFESSIONAL

Perl is a programming language of growing significance in the world of software development. Many professionals should learn it, so that they can correctly recognize applications for which it is the best language choice and so that they can use it in those areas in which it has become virtually essential: CGI and systems administration. This book could be used in self-taught mode, although some instruction should be helpful.

CHAPTER 1

Introduction

The intent of this chapter is to introduce the reader to just enough information about the Perl language to induce him or her into reading and studying the rest of the book and thereby becoming Perl literate. We do this by first describing the origins and general nature of Perl. We then briefly discuss the importance of Perl for CGI programming. Next, we introduce a few of the important characteristics of Perl and follow this with a short example program. Following the program, each of the statements of the program are briefly described.

1.1 WHAT PERL IS

Perl includes some of the most powerful constructs from a collection of predecessor programming languages and introduces a few new constructs of its own. The result is a language of great expressive power and flexibility. Except for those whose only software development interests lie with very large systems, most programmers should be interested in learning what Perl has to offer.

Perl began as a relatively modest programming language meant to extend the capabilities of the text editor `sed` and the text file processing utility `awk`. It was designed to write short programs to process text files, using elaborate and powerful pattern matching techniques, and then produce reports of the results of that processing. Perl soon evolved to include many of the features of the UNIX shell languages, `sh` and `csh`. Among these are capabilities for process creation and destruction, which help make Perl useful for system administration. Then the ability to use sockets was added, allowing Perl to be used as a networking language, supporting communication with other processes and other computers. More recently, Perl has acquired support for modules and object-oriented programming. Like other living languages, Perl is still evolving and growing, as this book is being written. The code in this book was developed and tested (at least minimally) using version 5.005 of Perl.

Perl is an acronym for *Practical extraction and report language*, although it has also been accused of being an acronym for *Pathologically eclectic rubbish lister*. From its first release (version 1.000) in 1987 and until mid-1994, the design and implementation of Perl were done by one very ambitious, gifted, and altruistic person, Larry Wall. The continued evolution of the language and its implementation are now being carried on by several other ambitious, gifted, and altruistic people.

Perl's ancestry places it in the gap between the shell utilities and high-level programming languages. Initially, this niche was small, but through the evolution and growth of Perl, it has grown to significant size. Perl has long since gone beyond being just a language for UNIX system administration and text processing. It has become the language of choice for a large number of other small- to medium-sized application programming tasks. It is the most popular language for Common Gateway Interface programming for the World Wide Web, as discussed in Section 1.3. Like most other popular contemporary programming languages, Perl has a collection of tools (profilers, debuggers, and syntax-directed editors) that together provide a modern software development environment. Perl has joined the relatively small collection of general-purpose programming languages that are both well supported and widely used.

Perl is, in a sense, a simple language—a beginner can write small but useful programs in it shortly after seeing it for the first time. But it is also a complex language, providing the richness and power that can be used to create programs that perform sophisticated tasks. Perl is made easier to learn by having borrowed most of its syntax from languages that are familiar to most programmers. Perl code looks a bit like C and a bit like sh and a bit like awk. If you know one or more of those languages, you will not find it difficult to learn Perl. If you don't, don't worry. You will still find Perl relatively easy to learn, and this book does not assume that you know any particular programming language (although you are expected to be familiar with programming in *some* high-level language).

Some Perl detractors think programs in Perl are obscure and weird, and it is certainly possible to write obfuscated programs in it. However, with a bit of programming discipline and a few simple standards, Perl programs can be as readable as those in practically any other popular programming language.

Although Perl began as a UNIX tool, it has spread to many non-UNIX systems and its popularity increased dramatically in the 1990s for several reasons. It is easily the most portable systems programming language. Some software development that was formally done under UNIX is now being done under non-UNIX systems. The programmers who made this transition have found comfort in that using Perl under those non-UNIX systems gives them the feeling that some of the UNIX culture came with them. Finally, Perl is easily obtained, free, and it is available for all popular computing platforms.

Many Perl programmers believe it is a language in which programming is not only relatively easy, but also fun. However, programming language theorists probably find little to love in Perl. "The language is intended to be practical (easy to use, efficient, complete), rather than beautiful (tiny, elegant, minimal)."[1]

---

[1] Perl manual, perl section, p. 2–3.

Many Perl users and many authors who write about Perl refer to collections of Perl statements as scripts. The next section explains the basis for this and also provides the rational for this book referring to these as programs.

1.2 SCRIPTS VERSUS PROGRAMS

Early operating systems for time-shared computers included small collections of commands that could be typed at a terminal and interpreted one at a time by a command interpreter program, which provided an interface to the operating system. Many of these commands were concerned with file manipulation. Programmers soon found it necessary to repeatedly type the same sequences of these commands. To avoid this tedious task, the commands were put in files and a way was developed to specify that the commands in a file be interpreted. Rather than calling the contents of these files programs, which they were not, they were called *scripts*. The first command language in UNIX was called shell (sh). The shell language, along with its later variations, such as csh and ksh, soon acquired some features that made them look more like programming languages. However, code in these languages continued to be interpreted by the operating system command interpreter.

Perl evolved, in part, from the shell languages. So, programs in Perl were and often are called scripts. However, Perl differs from the shell languages in that its scripts are first compiled into an intermediate language before they are interpreted. The compiler checks for a wide variety of certain and potential errors in the Perl program. This compilation makes the execution process of Perl similar to many other languages in which one writes programs, for example, Java. Collections of statements in these languages are never called scripts; they are programs.

We have no quarrel with those who call Perl programs scripts. However, we prefer to call them programs, and we will throughout this book. We believe Perl is not only a full-fledged programming language, but a powerful and flexible language of some import.

The use of Perl for internet programming is an important reason for its rapid rise in popularity.

1.3 CGI PROGRAMMING IN PERL

By 1995, a significant number of people were creating pages for the World Wide Web. Many of these people soon discovered that frequently there were things they wanted to have displayed on a page that could not be placed there using a markup language such as HTML—some more powerful approach must be used. The obvious solution was to turn to programs written in a general programming language. The most common examples of things that could not be handled by HTML are retrieving and displaying information from databases and interactions with the browser user. Because databases naturally are stored on the Web server (rather than a client), among other reasons, programs to do these things should reside there. So, it evolved that software would reside on the server, be enacted by a browser on a client system when requested by the HTML it was interpreting, and the results would be returned to the browser (in the form of

HTML) to be displayed for the user. An interface that supported this process was subsequently developed. This protocol or interface between the HTML on the client and the software on the server is called the Common Gateway Interface (CGI). Consequently, the development of such software was (and is) called CGI programming.

Initially, much of the CGI programming was done in the various shell languages, at least one of which is always present in UNIX systems. (Web servers, at least in the early days of the Web, usually ran on UNIX systems.) However, three problems with the shell languages for this use soon became evident. First, because there are several incompatible dialects of shell languages, Web pages that used a particular shell language are sometimes difficult to port to other UNIX systems. Second, for some kinds of programming tasks, such as text manipulation, which is common in CGI programming, the shell languages are cumbersome to use. Finally, the relatively slow speed of execution of shell languages made them less attractive for CGI applications. For these reasons, CGI programmers began to use high-level languages. Virtually any high-level language can be used for CGI programming. The features that are most commonly needed for this kind of programming are text manipulation, access to operating system environment variables, and interfacing to system utilities, databases, and other software packages. With these in mind, Perl has the following advantages for CGI programming:

- It is easy to port among all common Web server platforms.
- It is relatively easy to learn enough Perl to write CGI applications.
- System functions are built into Perl, greatly simplifying their use.
- Perl provides direct access to operating system environment variables.
- Perl has extensions that allow simple interfacing to non-Perl systems, such as the Oracle database system.

For these reasons, Perl has become the most widely used language for CGI programming. Because of this popularity, Lincoln Stein developed a module, CGI.pm, that includes Perl functions for the most common CGI programming tasks. CGI.pm is free and easy to use. Both CGI programming in Perl and the use of CGI.pm are discussed in Chapter 9.

Perl evolved around a number of interesting and powerful language design concepts. These provide a means of quickly introducing the essential flavor of the language.

1.4 CENTRAL CHARACTERISTICS OF PERL

Some knowledge of the fundamental characteristics of Perl provides a framework in which learning the language should be easier. One drawback of this discussion is that we must use some terms and ideas that are only fully defined later in the book. Bear with us here, for it is well worth the inconvenience.

Implicit variables.   Implicit variables are variables that are defined by the language implementation, rather than the user. Most high-level languages do not provide implicit variables that are accessible by the user. Their only implicit variables are the temporary variables created by the compiler for expression evaluation. Assembly languages often use registers as implicit variables. There are several operations in Perl that have optional operands. When the operand of such an operator is omitted, an implicit variable is used. The use of implicit variables is a programmer convenience, and it makes programs a bit shorter.

Interchangeability of functions and operators.   In most high-level languages, language-defined operators and functions are distinct categories of language features. In Perl, this distinction is blurred to the point where in many cases the difference is irrelevant. Specifically, Perl includes list operators in which the operator is followed by a list of operands. In other cases, it is convenient to enclose the operands of such an operator in parentheses, making it look like a function call. In other cases, it is convenient to omit the parentheses around the parameters in a function call, making it look like an operator and its operands. In Perl, the programmer has this choice.

Numbers are numbers.   Most programming languages provide several numeric data types and separate operations (often supported directly by hardware) for values of those types. Perl, however, has only one numeric data type, which is the same as the `double` type of languages such as C, C++, and Java. Numeric literals are all implicitly converted to this type, and most numeric operations are of this type.

Variables are implicitly declared.   In most modern programming languages, all variables must be explicitly defined in the program. This is done to provide specific data types, the size of strings and arrays, and other attribute information about variables. In Perl, as in some predecessor languages such as BASIC, the type of a variable is inferred by the compiler, in most cases from the syntax of its name, and sometimes from the context of its appearance.

Strings and numbers.   Some Perl operators impose a context on their operands that may cause implicit type conversions of the values of those operands. A common example of this is when a number appears as the operand of a string operator, in which case the number is implicitly converted to a string. Likewise, when a string literal or variable whose value is a string appears as the operand of an arithmetic operator, the value will be implicitly converted to a number.

Scalar and list context.   In some situations in Perl, an array variable can appear as the operand of an operator that expects a scalar operand. In these cases, the array variable is interpreted to be the length of the array. Also, a scalar variable can appear where an array operand is expected. Here, the variable is treated as an array of one element. This is another case of language flexibility.

There is more than one way to do it.   This is the Perl slogan, if there is such a thing. As you will discover by reading this book, in many situations you have a choice in how a certain computation or process can be designed and coded. This is good because one of the techniques is often just a bit better in some way in a given situation. This also provides the opportunity for programmers to be a bit more creative in their programs. In addition, programmers beginning to learn Perl can use simple techniques without having to first learn the more complex and possibly more elegant alternatives.

No unnecessary limits.   Overall, Perl has been designed to avoid specific limitations wherever possible. For example, neither character strings nor arrays are defined to have specific sizes. They implicitly grow when necessary to accommodate the needs of the program. Of course, there are ultimate limitations, but they are imposed by the size of your computer's memory. These features contribute greatly to the power and flexibility of Perl.

To make use of this book, the reader obviously must have access to a Perl language system. You cannot learn any language without a great deal of practice using it.

1.5 HOW TO GET PERL

Perhaps the most accessible source of the Perl system is from the Comprehensive Perl Archive Network (CPAN) on the World Wide Web. In addition to providing the compiler/interpreter, CPAN has practically everything you ever wanted to know about Perl. CPAN is duplicated (mirrored) at a large number of sites around the world. The Web site www.perl.com has a multiplexor service that finds the nearest CPAN site *to you*. You request this service by visiting

        http://www.perl.com/CPAN/

If you would rather choose a mirror site from a list, access the following Web site:

        http://www.perl.com/CPAN/SITES.html

Then you can get files from the distribution list located at that site.

There are several subdirectories under CPAN, the four most commonly useful are

doc   This directory contains Perl documentation, such as the Perl manual pages (manpages), in ASCII, HTML, PostScript, and Perl's own documentation format, Plain Old Documentation (POD), as well as "Frequently Asked Questions" (FAQs) and some other documents.

src   This directory has the source code files for the standard distribution of the Perl system. The current production version of Perl is found in src/stable.tar.gz (a UNIX-style tar archive compressed by GNU zip (gzip)) and src/stable.zip (a PC-style Zip archive).

ports   This directory contains subdirectories and symbolic links for implementations of Perl that are not directly supported by the standard distribution.

scripts   This is a collection of example Perl programs from many different sources.

For Windows platforms, the simplest way to get Perl is in object version, available from ActiveState, which produced the port to those systems. The Web site address is

        http://www.activestate.com/ActivePerl/default.htm

The best reference material on the current version of Perl is the manual, or as it is often called, the manpages, found in the doc subdirectory under CPAN. The manpages are also included in the standard source distribution. Perl has a very active newsgroup, comp.lang.perl.misc, which has a continually changing list of questions and often multiple answers and comments regarding Perl questions and observations. Also, there is a journal devoted to Perl, The Perl Journal. Information about this journal can be found at http://tpj.com.

1.6 AN EXAMPLE

One way to jump start into a new programming language is to look at an example program and an explanation of its statements. The sample program that follows illustrates some of the commonly used features of Perl. It is meant to give you a first look at Perl and these features before we begin a detailed description of the language. The program produces a report based on its analysis of an employee information file. The detailed specification is given in the initial documentation (comments) of the program. The line numbers in circles on the left margin are not part of the program. The narration following the program refers to these line numbers.

```
# salaries-    An example program to illustrate some of the features and
               the
#              flavor of Perl
#   Input:     A file of lines of employee data, where each line has the
#              form
#                 name:age:department code:salary
#   Output:    1. The names of all employees whose names end with "son"
#              2. Percentage of employees over 44 years old
#              3. Average salary of employees over 44 years old
#              4. An alphabetical list of employees who are over 44
#                    years old and who have salaries less than $35,000
①    open(EMPLOYEES, "employees") || die "Can't open employees $!";
②    print "Names that end in 'son'\n\n";

     # Loop to read and process the records of the employees file

③    while (<EMPLOYEES>){
④        $total_employees++;
⑤        chomp;

     # Split the record into its fields

⑥        ($name, $age, $dept, $salary) = split(/:/);

     # If the name ends in 'son', print it

⑦        if ($name =~ /son$/) {
⑧            print "$name \n";
⑨        }

     # If the employee is over 44, count him or her and add his or her
     #  salary to the sum

⑩        if ($age > 44) {
⑪          $over_44++;
⑫          $salary_sum += $salary;

     # If the salary is < 35,000, put the employee's name and salary into
     #  a hash table

⑬          if ($salary < 35_000) {
⑭            $sublist{$name}> = $salary;
⑮          }
⑯        }
⑰    }

     # If there was at least one employee, process the results

⑱    if ($total_employees > 0) {
     # If there was at least one employee over 44

⑲        if ($over_44 > 0) {
```

```
          # Compute and print the % of employees over 44 and their average
          #  salary

②⓪           $percent = 100 * $over_44 / $total_employees;
②①           print "\nPercent of employees over 44 is: $percent \n";
②②           $avg = $salary_sum / $over_44;
②③           print "Average salary of employees over 44 is: $avg \n";
②④           print "Sorted list of employees over 44",
②⑤                   " with salaries < \$35,000 \n";

          # Sort and print the names of the employees over 44

②⑥           @sorted_names = sort(keys(%sublist));
②⑦           print "\nName \t\t Salary\n";

②⑧           foreach $name (@<sorted_names) {
②⑨              print "$name \t \$$sublist{$name)> \n";
③⓪           }
③①        }
③②     else {
③③         print "There are no employees over 44 \n";
③④        }
③⑤  }
③⑥  else {
③⑦      print "There were no employees\n";
③⑧  }
```

These paragraphs briefly describe the actions of the statements of this program.
The first nine lines are documentation for the program. Our preferred style is to
begin all programs with the name of the program, a brief description, and a detailed description of its expected input and output. The pound sign (#) begins a comment. The end
of the line terminates the comment.

Line 1 attempts to open a file named employees and connect that file to the filehandle, EMPLOYEES. A filehandle is a name in a program used to refer to an external
source of data, in this case a file. The || specifies a logical OR operator. The second half
of this line is a die operator, which is executed only if the open fails. When executed, die
displays its operand literal string and terminates the program. So, this line attempts to
open a file, but if the file is not successfully opened, the program dies. The $! at the end
of the string operand of die is an implicit variable that is set to the error number of the
specific error that occurred during the open operation.

Line 2 displays a header for the first output of the program.

Line 3 is a while statement with an odd control expression. <EMPLOYEES> is an
input operator that reads a line of text from the file associated with the filehandle,
EMPLOYEES. The line is put in the implicit variable, $_. If the read operation succeeds in
getting a string of characters, the while condition is true. If the read encounters the
EOF marker, the while condition is false and the loop terminates.

Line 4 increments the scalar variable, $total_employees. Note that scalar variables are implicitly declared and initialized to undef, which is interpreted as zero when treated as a number.

Line 5 is the naked operator, chomp, which removes the end-of-line character(s) from $_. $_ is used as the default operand of chomp when none is given.

Line 6 uses the split function to separate the input string into four substrings, based on the colon separator character, and places the individual substrings into the four variables specified on the left side.

Line 7 tests whether the value of $name ends with the string, "son". If so, the name is displayed. Notice that even though there is only one statement in the "then"part of this statement, in Perl it must be delimited with braces.

Line 10 tests whether the value of $age is greater than 44. If so, the statements in the following brace-delimited statement sequence are chosen for execution.

Line 11 increments $over_44.

Line 12 adds $salary to $salary_sum.

Line 13 tests whether $salary is less than 35000 (note that Perl allows underscores to be used in numbers to increase their readability). If so, a new pair is added to the associative array, or hash, named $sublist. The new pair consists of $name and $salary. A hash is an array in which values are stored by keys, which are string values, rather than by numeric indices, or positions. The keys are stored as the odd-numbered elements of the array, if it is thought of as a simple array of scalars.

Line 18 tests whether $total_employees is greater than 0. If so, the statements in the following brace-delimited statement sequence are chosen for execution.

Line 19 tests whether there were any employees over 44. If so, the following brace-delimited sequence of statements are chosen for execution.

Line 20 computes the percentage of employees who were over 44.

Line 21 displays the result of the computation in line 20.

Line 22 computes the average salary for those over 44.

Line 23 displays the result of the computation in line 22.

Lines 24 and 25 display a label for the sorted list output. Notice that the literal dollar sign required a preceding backslash. This is because a nonbackslashed dollar sign is the beginning character of a scalar variable name.

Line 26 specifies several complex operations. First, the keys function returns the key part (first element) of each ordered pair in the hash named %sublist, which was constructed in line 14. The result of this is given to the sort operator, which does what its name suggests. This sorted list of keys is put in the array named @sorted_names.

Line 28 is a loop construct statement that takes the elements from the array `@sorted_names`, one for each loop iteration, assigning each name to `$name`.

Line 29 displays the name from the sorted list, along with the salary for that person, which is retrieved from the hash `$sublist`. The first dollar sign before `sublist` is to specify a literal dollar sign in the output. The second dollar sign is the first character in the variable name, `$sublist`.

Line 33 displays its message. This is the "else" part of the test of whether there were any employees over `44`.

Line 37 displays its message. This is the "else" part of the test of whether there was at least one employee.

1.7 SUMMARY

Perl began as an extended combination of `sed` and `awk`, but now has features and concepts borrowed from a number of diverse programming languages, along with a few ideas of its own. Perl is a powerful and widely used tool for a variety of different programming tasks. Perl is available free for all currently popular computers and operating systems.

CGI programming is a natural application for Perl, primarily because of its high level of portability, its powerful text manipulation facilities, its intimate connections to operating systems, and the relative ease with which enough of it can be learned to be useful for such programming.

There are a number of fundamental features that dominate the design of Perl. Among the most important of these are the implicit declarations of variables, the use of implicit variables, the interchangeability of functions and operators, and the idea of scalar and list contexts of operations.

Perl is available from CPAN, the main Perl distribution point. It is free and easy to obtain. Information about Perl, from examples to extensive documentation, is also available from CPAN. Perl is a powerful programming language that is easy, and many would say fun, to use.

1.8 EXERCISES

1. Access the `perl.com` Web site and peruse the HTML version of the Perl manpages, just to familiarize yourself with the available Perl language information.
2. If you have access to a system that includes an implementation of Perl, type `perl-v` at the operating system command prompt to determine the version number of that implementation.

CHAPTER 2

Scalar Types, Expressions, and Simple Input and Output

This chapter introduces the fundamental constructs of Perl, which form the basis of all Perl programs. With these constructs, including scalar literals and variables, expressions, assignment statements, and simple input and output, one can write complete albeit simple programs. Therefore, this chapter provides the language foundation on which the rest of Perl sits. Without a solid understanding of the basics, the discussion of the remaining Perl language constructs is virtually impossible.

We begin with a description of Perl's scalar literals. A literal is an instance of a data value that appears in a program.

2.1 SCALAR LITERALS

The simplest form of data in Perl is scalar. Scalar literals are single values of one of the three kinds: numbers, character strings, or references. Numeric and character string literals are discussed in the following two subsections. References, which are memory addresses, are discussed in Chapter 5.

2.1.1 NUMERIC LITERALS

Most computers provide hardware support for several numeric data types and most programming languages provide data types that correspond to those hardware-supported types. The Perl view of numeric data is quite different from that of most other

11

common programming languages—by default most numeric data in Perl programs are represented in a single data type, double-precision floating point. All floating-point values are stored as a fraction and an exponent, similar to scientific notation. Many languages provide two floating-point data types, standard and double precision. The double-precision floating-point type stores a much larger range of values than the standard floating-point type. Most operations on numeric values in Perl are done in its double-precision floating-point type.

It is possible to instruct the compiler to use integer arithmetic operations, but because that is not often done, we do not discuss it. However, the modulus operator, the repetition operator, and the bitwise operators described in Sections 2.3.1, 2.3.3, and 2.9, respectively, always cause their numeric operands to be converted to integer values before performing their operations.

Numeric literals can appear in any of the three forms: a string of digits with no decimal point and no exponent, a string of digits with a decimal point, or either of those two forms followed by an exponent. An exponent begins with an E or an e, and is followed by a possibly signed integer literal. All of the following are legal Perl numeric literals:

```
37      3.7     .37     37.     3E7     3e7     .3E7     3.E7    3E-7
```

Integer literals can be specified in hexadecimal (base 16) by preceding them with 0x or 0X. They can be specified in octal (base 8) by preceding them with a zero. For example,

```
0x2aff     0xAA3
```

are hexadecimal numeric literals, and

```
0276       077
```

are octal numeric literals.

Underscore characters can be embedded in numeric literals to make them more readable. For example,

```
3_296_429
```

specifies the value 3,296,429, or simply 3296429.

2.1.2 STRING LITERALS

There are two kinds of string literals in Perl, those delimited by single quotes (') and those delimited by double quotes (").[1] Two different delimiters are used because they each specify a different context for how the strings they delimit are interpreted.

The null string, which has no characters and a length of zero, is denoted by both of the following:

```
' '        " "
```

---

[1]These are also called apostrophes and quotation marks, but it is common in computing literature to call them single quotes and double quotes.

2.1.2.1 SINGLE-QUOTED STRING LITERALS

The simplest string literals are those delimited by single quotes, which can include typed newlines if the string literal crosses one or more line boundaries.[2] String literals that are delimited by single quotes cannot include single quotes or escape sequence characters (for example, \t for tab).

The backslash character can have special meaning in string literals. The most common use of backslash in a single-quoted string literal is to allow a single quote to be embedded in the string. To do this, the single quote is preceded immediately by a backslash, which serves in this context to tell the compiler the single quote is to be included in the string, rather than being used to signify the end of the string. A backslash followed by any character except a single quote or a backslash in a single-quoted string literal is considered a backslash.[3] Following are examples of single-quoted string literals:

```
'poopsie'
'apples are good\t'          - Has \ and t as its last two characters (not a tab)
'Wouldn\'t it be loverly?'   - The first word has eight characters
'good                        - Eight characters,
bye'                           including the embedded newline
```

It should be noted that in this last example, the length of the literal is considered to be eight, regardless of whether newline is represented as one or two characters.

If a string literal contains several single quotes and you want to use the single-quoted form, a different delimiter can be specified and used, rather than backslashing all of the embedded single quotes. For example, consider the string

```
'can\'t, won\'t, wouldn\'t ever!'
```

We could specify that ^ is the delimiter for this string literal by preceding the string with q^ and typing ^ after the string. This would obviate the need to backslash the embedded single quotes, because they are not used as delimiters in this case. The preceding example would then appear as

```
q^can't, won't, wouldn't ever!^
```

If a character that has a natural mate is used as the left delimiter on a string literal, its mate is used for the delimiter on the right end. The four mated pairs are parentheses, braces ({ }), brackets ([ ]), and angle brackets (< >). For example,

```
q(Is Perl more fun than baseball?)
q[Well, maybe not.]
```

---

[2]A newline is specified on the keyboard with the enter or return key. On UNIX systems, newline is represented by a line-feed character (ASCII code 10); on some other systems, it is represented by two characters, a carriage return and a line feed (ASCII codes 10 and 13).

[3]If you happen to have two adjacent backslashes in a single-quoted string literal, the first one makes the second one literal, so you only get one, which is the same as if you only put one in the string.

2.1.2.2 DOUBLE-QUOTED STRING LITERALS

Double-quoted string literals are different from single-quoted literals in two ways: 1) They can include escape sequences to code special characters and 2) variable names that appear in them are interpolated (converted to their values). Variable interpolation is discussed in Section 2.2.

The escape sequences, or multiple character sequences, for the special characters are shown in Table 2.1.

As an example of a string literal with embedded special characters, consider the following:

```
"Quantity \t Price \t Total \n\n"
```

Obviously, a string such as this is meant to be displayed or printed.

If you want to have an embedded double quote in a double-quoted string literal, it must be preceded by a backslash, as in

```
"The dog replied, \"wuff!\""
```

When a double-quoted string literal is typed on two lines, it includes an embedded newline (as is the case with single-quoted string literals).

Double-quoted string literals can specify a delimiter by preceding it with qq, as in

```
qq*"Definitely not!", she answered.*
```

Before discussing interpolation of variables whose names appear in double-quoted strings, we obviously must introduce variables. Because this chapter is restricted to scalar values and operations, the kind of variables we discuss here are those for storing scalar values.

Table 2.1

ESCAPE SEQUENCES FOR SPECIAL CHARACTERS.

Escape Sequence	Meaning
\n	newline
\r	return
\t	tab
\f	formfeed
\b	backspace
\v	vertical tab
\a	bell
\e	escape
\cC	any control character, C
\\	backslash
\"	double quote
\l	makes the next letter lowercase
\L	makes all letters until \E lowercase
\u	makes the next letter uppercase
\U	makes all letters until \E uppercase
\E	terminates \L and \U
\ddd	any three-digit octal value
\xhh	any two-digit hex value

2.2 SCALAR VARIABLES

A variable has two components, a name and the address of a memory location with which the variable is associated. The value of a variable is stored in its associated memory location. A scalar variable is one that stores scalar values. All scalar variables have names with the same syntactic form, a dollar sign followed by a letter, possibly followed by a string of letters, digits, and underscores. There is no length limit, and all characters in a name are significant. The following two names are distinct:[4]

```
$supercalifragilisticexpialadocious
$supercalifragilisticexpialadoces
```

The letters in names are case sensitive, so `$Rose` is not the same as `$ROSE` or `$rose` or `$RoSe`. It is a Perl convention, as it is in several other programming languages, that user-defined variable names do not use uppercase letters. Names using only uppercase letters are reserved for variables whose values never change (sometimes called constants). We prefer underscores over embedded uppercase letters, so we like `$sum_of_squares` better than `$sumOfSquares`, although that is a matter of taste.

Scalar variables are not defined to have a specific type. In fact, they are often not explicitly defined at all. As stated earlier, all scalar variables can store numbers, strings, or references to other memory locations. The mere appearance of a scalar variable in a program causes the compiler to implicitly define it. All implicitly defined variables in a Perl program are global, or have global scope, meaning they are visible in the whole program. There are scalar variable declarations in Perl, but we discuss them only when they become relevant, which is in Chapter 6.

Variable interpolation is illustrated by the following example, where we assume the value of `$name is "bob"`:

```
"Apples are good for $name"
```

is interpreted as

```
"Apples are good for bob"
```

If we did not want `$name` to be interpolated, we would backslash the `$`, as in

```
"Apples are good for \$name"
```

Of course, we could also use single quotes to avoid interpolation.

When a double-quoted string literal has an embedded single-quoted string literal, or vice versa, the outer quotes determine the nature of the string. For example, in

```
"The boy sent the message, 'Help, send $money'"
```

`$money` is interpolated, even though it is in a single-quoted string. Furthermore, in

```
'The boy sent the message, "Help, send $money"'
```

`$money` is not interpolated.

If you want an alphanumeric character to appear immediately to the right of the value of a scalar variable that is interpolated in a double-quoted string, you must put

---

[4]Except for six missing hypens, the first of these is the "correct" spelling.

braces (`{ }`) around the variable's name.[5] For example, if `$day` stores the string `"Mon"`, the value of

```
"Today is ${day}day";
```

is

```
"Today is Monday"
```

You may think the dollar signs look silly and these implicit declarations are sloppy and/or dangerous, but there is method to this madness. First, variable names are the most important class of Perl nouns (names of things), and they look different from Perl verbs (words that specify some action). This is not a new idea. In German, all nouns begin with uppercase letters to make them look different from words that are not nouns. Second, when the name of a scalar variable appears in a double-quoted string literal, its unique name form allows it to be recognized as the name of a scalar and its value can be interpolated into the string (as discussed in Section 2.1.2). Finally, if new reserved words are added to Perl in the future, they will not collide with variable names in existing Perl programs.

Perl includes a large number of implicit variables, many of which are scalars. Implicit variables are often used as default operands for certain operators and default parameters for certain predefined functions. Implicit scalar variable names begin, of course, with dollar signs. We will discuss the most commonly used implicit variable, which is named `$_`, in Section 2.3. Other categories of variables, such as arrays, also use a special character to begin their names. Now we are ready to look at scalar operators and expressions.

2.3 SCALAR OPERATORS

Perl includes a rich set of operators. This section describes the most commonly used operators for scalar data, as well as some functions that perform operations on string values. Recall from Chapter 1 that operators and functions are closely related in Perl.

2.3.1 ARITHMETIC OPERATORS

Perl includes binary arithmetic operators (operators with two operands) for addition (+), subtraction (-), multiplication (*), division (/), exponentiation (**), and modulus, or remainder after division (%). The following examples illustrate the modulus operator:

```
4 % 2    is 0  (i.e., the remainder of dividing 4 by 2 is 0)
7 % 2    is 1
18 % 4   is 2
```

If either operand of the modulus operator happens to have a noninteger value, such as `7.86`, that value is implicitly converted to an integer by truncation before the operation is performed. Truncation simply removes the fractional part, so `7.86` would be

---

[5]If you put the character immediately after the variable's name, it would be considered part of the name.

truncated to 7. With all of the other arithmetic operators, including **, operands with integer values are implicitly converted to double-precision floating-point values. Implicit conversions are called *coercions*. For example, in

```
5 / 2
```

although both operands are integer literals, they are coerced to `double`, and a `double` division operation takes place, producing 2.5. In many other programming languages, the value of this expression would be 2, because there would be no coercion to `double` and an integer operation would be done, resulting in the truncation of the fractional part of the quotient.

Perl also provides unary plus and minus operators, along with unary increment (++), and unary decrement (--). The increment and decrement operators are fundamentally different from the others, because their operands must be variables and because they have side effects. For example, the expression

```
$sum++ (means the same as $sum = $sum + 1)
```

not only fetches the value of the variable `$sum` and adds one, it also replaces the old value of `$sum` with this new value. So, these unary operators are related to the assignment statement, which is discussed in Section 2.5.

The increment and decrement operators can be either prefix (appearing before their operands) or postfix (appearing after their operands). When they appear in expressions with other operators, the meaning of these unary operators depends on whether they are prefix or postfix. For example, in the expression

```
++$total * 3
```

the value of `$total` is first incremented. The new value is then used as the first operand of the multiplication. So, if the value of `$total` is 3, the value of the expression is 12. On the other hand, in the expression

```
$total++ * 3
```

the old value of `$total` is used as the operand of the multiplication. In this case, the value of the expression, assuming the value of `$total` is 3, is 9. But `$total` is still incremented as a side effect of evaluating the expression. Unary decrement behaves similarly.

2.3.2 NUMERIC EXPRESSION EVALUATION ORDER

Every programming language that allows expressions with more than one operator must also have rules that dictate the order in which those operators are evaluated. Among most common programming languages, the rules that govern expression evaluation order are similar. The most basic of such rules are called *precedence rules*. They specify a level of precedence or importance for each operator. For example, addition usually has a lower level of precedence than multiplication. So, in the expression

```
$a + $b * 2
```

the multiplication is performed before the addition. Notice that in most cases, performing the addition first would result in a different expression value.

When an expression has two adjacent operators[6] that are either the same or are have the same precedence, another set of rules, called *associativity rules*, dictate the evaluation order. These specify either left-to-right or right-to-left associativity for each operator. Consider an expression that has two operators that have equal precedence. Left-to-right, or simply left associativity means the operation specified by the left operator is performed before the operation specified by the right operator. Likewise, right-to-left, or right associativity means the operation specified by the right operator is performed first. For example, division is left associative, so in the expression

    $a / $b / 2

the left division is done first. So, if the values of $a and $b are 8 and 2, respectively, the value of this expression would be 2. (If division were right associative, the value would be 8.) However, in the expression

    $a ** $b ** 2

the right exponentiation operator is evaluated first, because the exponentiation operator is right associative.

In any expression parentheses can be used to force the evaluation order. So, in

    $a / ($b / 2)

the right division is done first. In this case, the value of the expression would be 8. Likewise, in

    $a * ($b + $c)

the addition operator would be performed first, even though multiplication has higher precedence than addition.

The precedence and associativity of the numeric operators are shown in Table 2.2, in which the operators appearing first have the highest precedence. The "none" associativity means two of the nonassociative operators cannot appear in an expression separated only by a single operand. For example, ++$a-- is invalid (in addition to being silly).

A variable that has not been explicitly assigned a value has the value undef. This value is assigned to the variable when the compiler implicitly defines it, which happens when it finds the first appearance of that variable in the program. When undef is inter-

---

Table 2.2

OPERATOR PRECEDENCE AND ASSOCIATIVITY FOR THE COMMON NUMERIC OPERATORS (++ AND -- HAVE THE HIGHEST PRECEDENCE)

Operator	Associativity
++ --	none
unary -	right
**	right
* / %	left
binary + -	left

---

[6]Two operators are considered adjacent if they are separated by a single operand.

preted as a number, its value is 0. Therefore, it is neither a syntax nor a run-time error to have a variable in an expression that has `undef` as its value. `undef` also may be returned by some operators and functions.

The order of evaluation of operands of an operator in an expression in Perl is unspecified. The compiler is allowed to choose the order in which operands are evaluated in each expression.[7] This leads to expressions whose value cannot be predetermined; that is, their value may depend on the particular implementation on which the expressions are evaluated. For example, in the expressions

```
$a++ * $a--
```

suppose `$a` has the value 3 before the expression is evaluated. If the left operand is evaluated first, the value of the whole expression is 12. If the right operand is evaluated first, the value is 6. (Recall that the increment and decrement operators have higher precedence than multiplication.) It is obviously not a good idea to have the value of any expression depend on the order of evaluation of operands. So, any expression similar to the one above should be avoided.

2.3.3 STRING OPERATORS

The first thing that must be understood about Perl strings is that they are *not* stored as arrays of characters, as strings are in many other programming languages. Therefore, individual characters in a string cannot be accessed as elements of an array, through subscripting. Individual characters and substrings are accessible only through predefined functions, some of which are described in Section 2.3.4.

String catenation[8] is specified with the dot operator `(.)`. In a Perl expression, it is never legal to have two string literals and/or variables with string values appear next to each other. Therefore, the catenation operator cannot be implicit. For instance, consider the following example, in which we assume that the value of `$str` is `"Happy"`:

```
$str " Holidays!"
```

This code is invalid. Instead, we could have

```
$str . " Holidays!"
```

which results in the single string

```
"Happy Holidays!"
```

The values of the operands of the catenation operator are not affected by the catenation operation—the new string is exactly that, a new string.

The repetition operator, specified with a lowercase x, replicates its left string operand the number of times specified by its numeric right operand. For example,

```
"Happy Birthday! " x 3
```

creates the string

```
"Happy Birthday! Happy Birthday! Happy Birthday! "
```

---

[7]This choice is given to the compiler because some orders of operand evaluation are more efficient than others.

[8]Catenation means the same as concatenation, but requires less typing

The right operand of the repetition operator can be any arithmetic expression, but its value is coerced to an integer. The left operand can be any string expression. The repetition operator has higher precedence than the catenation operator. Therefore, the value of the string expression

```
"Happy " . "Birthday! " x 2
```

is

```
"Happy Birthday! Birthday! "
```

rather than

```
"Happy Birthday! Happy Birthday! "
```

When a scalar variable is used as a string but has the value undef, it is interpreted as the empty string, "".

Because the catenation and repetition operators are clearly not adequate for many useful string manipulation programs, Perl includes a collection of powerful functions that operate on strings.

2.3.4 STRING FUNCTIONS

This section describes the most commonly used predefined functions that perform operations on string values. Before discussing them, we briefly examine Perl functions.

A function in Perl is related to a function in mathematics, but only loosely. Perl functions compute and return values when called with the necessary parameters[9] The form of a function call is

function_name (actual parameter list)

The actual parameters are expressions that specify values to be sent to the function. The returned value of a function replaces, in effect, the call itself. In some cases, the value returned by a function is of no interest. When this is the case, the function call can appear by itself as a Perl expression, as in

```
fun(x)
```

In many cases, Perl's functions can be treated as either operators or functions. If you think of one of these as a function, you can delimit the actual parameters in a call to it with parentheses to make it look like a function call. If you think of one of these functions as an operator, you can simply list its operands after the operator.[10]

Suppose fun is a function that uses $_ as its default actual parameter (or operand). That is, the function uses $_ as its parameter value when it is enacted by a call that does not include an actual parameter. Such a call can be specified with either of the following two:

```
fun()
fun
```

---

[9] We call the values (or expressions) specified in function calls *actual parameters* and the parameters in the function definition *formal parameters*. Some other authors call them arguments and parameters, respectively.

[10] If the first parameter 1(or operand) happens to begin with a left parenthesis, then the whole list must be parenthesized, regardless of how you prefer to think of the operator/function.

Chapter 5 has a detailed discussion of user-written Perl functions.

Now we can discuss some of the predefined functions that operate on string values. Frequently we need to remove the last character from a specific string. The `chop` function does exactly this to its parameter string. For example, if the value of `$fruit` is `"apples"`,

    chop($fruit)

changes the value of `$fruit` to

    "apple"

and returns the removed character, `"s"`. Furthermore, if the value of `$fruit` is `"apples"`,

    chop($fruit) x 2

evaluates to

    "appleapple"

The primary operation of `chop` is exhibited through the side effect of changing the value of its parameter. One of the reasons we stated earlier that Perl functions are only loosely related to mathematical functions is this instance of changing parameters, which never happens in a mathematical function. Typically, the returned value from `chop` is ignored, and the call to `chop` is a complete expression. It makes little sense to call `chop` with a literal, as in

    chop("gumballs")

because there is no place to put the modified string value. Furthermore, why not write `"gumball"`, rather than calling a function.

One common use of `chop`, especially in older Perl programs, is to remove the newline character from a line that has been input from the keyboard or a text file. There are two problems with using chop for this: (1) If the string does not have a newline at the end, whatever character is last will be removed, and (2) although in UNIX systems newline is represented by a single character (a carriage return), in some non-UNIX systems, two characters are used for newline—a carriage return and a line feed. Because of the different ways newline is represented, it is better to consider *input record separators—* rather than newlines—where an input record separator is one character on some systems and two characters on other systems. Because of the potential problems with `chop`, Perl includes a function, `chomp`, that removes whatever the system uses for an input record separator, regardless of the number of characters it includes.[11] `chomp` returns the number of input record separators it removed. If `chomp` is used on a string that does not end with an input record separator, it does nothing to the string and returns zero. Therefore, `chomp` is used when you are not sure the string ends with an input record separator, even if you know the input record separator is a single character. We will always use `chomp` to remove input record separators in this book and recommend you do the same, because it makes the code more platform independent.

---

[11]Actually, Perl has an implicit variable, $\, that is initially set to the character or character pair that is used for the input record separator. In UNIX implementations, it is set to a carriage return character; in some other implementations, it is set to the two characters these systems use for the input record separator, a carriage return and a line feed. You could set $\ to whatever you want and use chomp to remove that from given strings.

Both `chop` and `chomp` use the implicit variable `$_` as the default parameter when none is specified. Both `chop` and `chomp` can take a list of strings as parameters. In these cases, `chop` removes the last character of each parameter and returns the character removed from the first parameter. For example, if the values of `$a`, `$b`, and `$c` are `"a"`, `"an"`, and `"ant"`, respectively, then

```
chop($a, $b, $c)
```

changes `$a` to `""`, `$b` to `"a"`, and `$c` to `"an"` and returns `"a"`. When given more than one parameter, `chomp` removes the input record separator from each line that has one and returns the total number of removed separators.

Although `chop` or `chomp` is needed to remove input record separators from string input, they are not needed with numeric input. All keyboard input is in the form of strings. Using a string in an expression (or as an actual parameter to a function) where a number is expected causes the string to be converted to a number. The conversion uses the input record separator as a delimiter for the end of the number, but otherwise ignores it. Therefore, when a number is input from the keyboard (or a text file), neither `chop` nor `chomp` need be used on that input.

We often must determine the number of characters in a string. The `length` function takes a string parameter and returns the number of characters in that string. For example, if the value of `$str` is `"apples"`,

```
length($str)
```

returns 6. Note that if there is an input record separator in the string given to length, it is counted as one character, regardless of whether it is actually one or two.[12]

Sometimes we have to translate the uppercase letters in a string to lowercase letters, or vice versa. All of the lowercase letters in a string can be converted to uppercase with the function `uc`. Likewise, for converting the uppercase letters in a string to lowercase, the function `lc` can be used. For example, if the value of `$str` is `"Apples are good for you. So is Perl."`,

```
lc($str)
```

returns `"apples are good for you. so is perl."`.

The `ord` function returns the numeric ASCII code for the first character of its parameter. For example,

```
ord("apples")
```

returns the ASCII code for `'a'`, which is 97.

Perl includes functions for converting strings that represent hexadecimal and octal numbers to numeric internal form. The `hex` function takes a string as a parameter, which it interprets as a string containing a hexadecimal number, and returns the value of the parameter number. For example,

```
hex("1F3")
```

returns the value 499 (the decimal value of the hex humber 1F3). If `hex` is not passed a parameter, `$_` is used.

---

[12]In some programming languages, string length operations do not count input operators at all.

If a string has an octal or hexadecimal number with the leading 0 or 0x, the oct function is used to convert its value to a number. If oct is given no parameter, $_ is used. The sprintf function can be used to do the inverse operation to that of hex. Section 2.6 describes sprintf.

Text processing often requires that a string be searched for a specific substring. Perl includes two functions for this task, index, which searches a string from left to right, and rindex, which does the same in the other direction. Both of these functions take two string parameters, the string to be searched and the searched-for string. Both return the character position, counting from zero on the left end, of the first character of the searched-for string. If the substring was not found, both functions return -1. Consider the following examples:

```
index("apples", "pp")  returns 1
rindex("apples", "pp") returns 1
index("apples", "p")   returns 1
rindex("apples", "p")  returns 2
index("apples", "q")   returns -1
```

Sometimes it is necessary to extract a substring at a particular position in a given string. This is often done after index or rindex has found a substring. The substr function takes a string and two numbers as parameters and does this sort of extraction, as in

```
substr($str, position, length)
```

The position parameter specifies the position of the first character to be extracted. The length parameter specifies the number of characters to be extracted. If the value of the second parameter is negative, the position is counted from the right, rather than the left. Consider the following examples, in which we assume the value of $str is "fruit juice":

```
substr($str, 0, 3)   returns "fru"
substr($str, 3, 5)   returns "it ju"
substr($str, -3, 3)  returns "ice"
```

The third parameter to substr is optional. If omitted, substr returns all characters from the specified position to the right end of the string.

Perl has a function for building new strings from two or more existing strings and one for taking strings apart, join and split, respectively. We discuss the join function here, but postpone describing the split function until Chapter 4, because it is often used with arrays. The join function call has the form

```
join Expression, List
```

where the Expression specifies a string, usually of one character, that is to be the separator between the parts of the new string. The second parameter specifies the list of strings to be joined together—for example,

```
join ':', $month, $day, $year;
```

Table 2.3

STRING FUNCTIONS

Function	Parameter	Operation
chop	string	removes and returns the last character
chomp	string	removes the trailing input record separator, if there is one
length	string	returns the length of its parameter
lc	string	converts any uppercase letters in the string to lowercase
uc	string	converts any lowercase letters in the string to uppercase
ord	string	returns the ASCII numeric code for the first given character
hex	string	converts the string to a hexadecimal number and returns it
oct	string	converts the string to an octal number and returns it
index	two strings	returns the position of the second parameter in the first
rindex	two strings	same as index, except it returns the position from the right
substr	a string and two numbers	extracts and returns a substring from the first number position to the second
join	a character and a list	joins the list of strings together into one string, separating them with the given character

If the null string is used as the separator, join simply catenates the strings together. In fact, this is the fastest way to do string catenation. The string functions discussed in this section are summarized in Table 2.3.

In writing Perl programs, it frequently happens that we write expressions that include operands of both of the two scalar data types: numbers and strings. Obviously, we must know how such expressions are interpreted.

2.4 MIXED-MODE EXPRESSIONS

When the two operands of a binary operator have different data types, the expression is called a *mixed-mode expression*. In this section, we discuss one particular kind of mixed-mode expression—that with one binary operator which has one numeric operand and one string operand.

In Perl, when a numeric value operand is used with a string operator, it is coerced to the string that would appear if its value were printed. When a string value appears as the operand of a numeric operator, it is coerced to a number. Leading white space and trailing nondigit characters are ignored in this conversion. So, " 2x" is converted to 2, and the 'x' is ignored. If the string does not include a number under these rules, the value 0 is used.

Consider the following examples, in which we assume the value of $str is " 32abc":

    7 + $str The value of $str is converted to 32, and the result is 39.
    7 . $str 7 is converted to "7", and the result is "7 32abc".
    - $str   The value of $str is converted to 32, and the result is -32.

If $str is "alpha32", the result of

    7 + $str

is 7, because, according to the preceding rules, since `$str` does not contain a number, the value zero is used.

The only situation in which the unary plus operator has any effect is when the operand is a string. In this case, the value is converted to a number. The coercion of a string to a number does not work for octal or hexadecimal literals. These must be converted using the `oct` function.

Perl provides no function or operator for explicitly converting the type of a value, such as the casts of C and its successors.

Now that we have described scalar literals, variables, and expressions, we can introduce the fundamental statement of Perl, the assignment statement.

2.5 ASSIGNMENT STATEMENTS

Assignment statements are the primary means of computation in most common programming languages.[13] They are, therefore, of central importance in any of these languages, including Perl.

2.5.1 THE SIMPLE ASSIGNMENT OPERATOR

The simple assignment operator, =, takes two operands: a target variable on the left and an expression on the right, as in the code

```
$average = $sum / $total;
$last_name = "van Beethoven";
$name = "Ludwig " . $last_name;
```

Notice that these statements are terminated by semicolons. Every Perl statement must be terminated by a semicolon, unless it is the last statement in a block. (See Chapter 3.)

As we stated earlier, variables have two components: an address and a value. The value of a variable is used when the variable appears as an operand in an expression. The address of a variable is used when the variable appears on the left side of an assignment. This has led to naming the value of a variable its *r-value* (for the *r*ight side of an assignment) and the address of a variable its *l-value* (for the *l*eft side of an assignment). The left side of an assignment must have an l-value. Literals cannot appear as the left sides of assignments because they do not have l-values.

An assignment operator produces a result, which is the assigned value. Because of this, an assignment statement can be used as an operand in an expression. The precedence of the assignment operator is lower than all of the operators discussed so far, and it is right associative. For example, consider the following statements:

```
$sum_a = $sum_b = $sum_c = 0;
$result = 17 * ($sum = $total_1 + $total_2);
```

In the first statement, the value 0 is first assigned to `$sum_c`, then to `$sum_b`, and finally to `$sum_a`. Because the meaning of such statements is less obvious, we do not

---

[13]The two categories of programming languages that do not base computation on assignment statements are the functional languages (for example, LISP) and the logic languages (such as Prolog).

recommend using them. In the second example, the embedded assignment statement is parenthesized to insure that it is evaluated before the multiplication. The right operand of the multiplication is the value of $sum *after* its assignment of the sum of $total_1 and $total_2.

The result of an assignment can be used as either the value of the assigned value or as the address of the target variable (a l-value or a r-value). For example, although chomp requires an operand with an l-value, we could have

```
chomp($str = $str1 . $str1);
```

In this example, it is the new value of $str that is chomped.

The existing type (numeric or string) of the value in a scalar variable is irrelevant when it is the target of an assignment. For example, we could have

```
$a = 17.38;
```

and later

```
$a = "Beethoven";
```

2.5.2 EXPRESSIONS AS STATEMENTS

So far we have discussed just one Perl statement form, the simple assignment. However, there is an intimate relationship between expressions and statements, which leads to a closely related second statement form, the expression. An expression can appear anywhere a statement can appear. For example, we could have

```
$a * $b - 1;
```

as a statement. Because the evaluation of this expression has no side effects (no variables have their values changed), it serves no purpose by itself. On the other hand, expressions with side effects, such as

```
$a++;
```

are useful as complete statements. We will consider such expressions to be assignment statements.

2.5.3 COMPOUND ASSIGNMENT OPERATORS

The frequency with which a certain kind of simple assignment statement appears in programs has led to an abbreviation of it in the C language and its descendants, including Perl. This common assignment statement form is

```
$whatever = $whatever operator operand
```

where the operator is any binary operator that is appropriate for $whatever and the operand. The abbreviation of this statement form uses a combination of the assignment operator and the other operator, which is then called a compound assignment operator, in the statement. The following code is illustrative:

```
$sum += $new_value;     # Same as $sum = $sum + $new_value;
$str .= "ing";          # Same as $str = $str . "ing";
$result **= 4;          # Same as $result = $result ** 4;
```

All of the binary arithmetic, string, and Boolean (see Chapter 3) operators in Perl can be used this way. (Recall that # begins a comment on any line and the end of the line terminates a comment.)

The precedence of the compound assignment operators is the same as that of the simple assignment operator, not that of the other operator. For example, `**=` has the same precedence as `=` (and `+=`), rather than that of `**`. Because of this, the compound assignment operators should only be used when the right side operand contains no operators. The problem that can occur in other cases is illustrated by the following example:

```
$a = 2;
$a *= 2 + 1;    # The new value of $a is 6 (+ is first)
```

Next, we discuss the processes of getting input from the keyboard and directing output to the screen.

2.6 SIMPLE KEYBOARD INPUT AND SCREEN OUTPUT

Although Perl programs often process data from files and write their output to files, keyboard input and screen output are also essential. Furthermore, a brief discussion of these simple processes allows us to write small but complete programs without getting into the details of file input/output. So, here is that brief discussion.

Files, including standard input (the keyboard) and standard output (the screen), are specified in programs with special variables called *filehandles*. The preassigned filehandle for standard input in Perl is STDIN. The preassigned filehandle for standard output is STDOUT.

2.6.1 KEYBOARD INPUT

Compared to other programming languages, getting a line from the keyboard (or a file) into a variable in a program is quite different in Perl. In Perl, an operator with a decidedly odd appearance is used. The operator is called the *line input operator*, or *angle operator*. The filehandle of the input file is placed in angle brackets. The angle brackets are the operator and the filehandle is the operand.[14] The expression `<STDIN>` reads keyboard input, up to, and including, an input record separator, and this string value replaces the appearance of `<STDIN>`.[15] If nothing has been typed when the call is executed, the `perl` interpreter waits.

Frequently, `<STDIN>` is the right side of an assignment to a scalar variable, as for example in the statement

```
$new_input = <STDIN>;
```

In many cases where the input will be used as a string, the input record separator is not wanted. So, a common idiom in Perl has the form of

```
chomp($new_input = <STDIN>);
```

When the end-of-file is found in the input, `<STDIN>` returns undef. The keyboard input that specifies end-of-file is system dependent. On UNIX systems, it is Control-D; on Windows 95 and NT, it is Control-Z; on a Macintosh, it is COMMAND-. (period).

---

[14] Should the line input operator be called an *outfix* operator?

[15] As we shall see in Chapter 4, the line input operator can read far more than a single line.

2.6.2 SCREEN OUTPUT

Output to the screen is as simple as input from the keyboard. It is specified with `print`, which can be considered either an operator or a function. There can be any number of parameters (or operands), all of which are strings. The filehandle for the screen is STDOUT. However, the default filehandle for print is STDOUT, so STDOUT need not be specified if that is what you want. Consider the following examples:

```
print "Isn't this fun?\n";
print("That may be an overstatement!\n");
print("The sum is: $sum", "\tThe average is: $average\n");
```

The last example works, because scalar variables are interpolated in quoted literal strings. We will always use the unparenthesized (operator) form of `print` in this book, but that is a matter of taste.

If a bit more control over output format is necessary, the `printf` function can be used. This function's first parameter is a string literal specification of the form of the output, including literal characters and format codes for the values of variables. This first parameter is called the *format code parameter*, or simply *control string*. The remaining parameters are the names of the variables whose values are to be output.

The format code for string values is %*n*s; for integer values is %*n*d; for floating-point values is %*n.m*f. In all three cases, *n* is an integer literal that specifies the number of spaces in which the value will be right justified. In the floating-point case, *m* is an integer literal that specifies the number of digits to the right of the decimal point which are to be displayed. All characters (apart from the format codes) in the format code parameter are copied as is to the output line, including spaces. Consider the following code:

```
$a = "apples";
$b = 173;
$c = 17.355;
printf "\$a, \$b, and \$c are: %7s %5d %6.2f \n", $a, $b, $c;
```

The output of this code is

```
$a, $b, and $c are: apples 173 17.36
```

The variable names in the format code parameter are preceded by backslashes to prevent them from being interpolated into the string. Notice that the value of `$c` was rounded, not truncated, to fit into the specified two digits to the right of the decimal point.

The preceding format codes we used all result in right justification. For example, the number `173` printed with `%5d` will be preceded by two spaces. We can specify left justification by placing a minus sign just after the `%` of the format code. So, if we print `173` with `%-5d`, the `173` is left justified and padded with two spaces on the right.

The form and semantics of the `printf` function are borrowed directly from C. More information on `printf` can be found in any textbook on that language.

The `sprintf` function is identical to `printf`, except `sprintf` returns its output, rather than sending it to standard output. `sprintf` is most often used for converting internal numeric values to strings. For example,

```
$sum = 427.56;
```

```
$str_sum = sprintf("%f6.1", $sum);
```

puts " 427.6" in $str_sum.

A word in a Perl program that cannot be interpreted any other way is taken to be a literal string. These are often called *bareword literals*. For example,

```
print goodbye, "\n";
```

displays goodbye. We do not recommend the use of barewords; if it is a literal string, delimit it. The use of barewords can be prohibited by including a use pragma in the program. (See Chapter 5.)

2.7 AN EXAMPLE

At long last we have reached the point where we can consider a simple, but complete program, using only language features we have explained. Of course, with the tiny bit of Perl we have covered, the example is necessarily trivial. It prompts the user to type a number, which is taken to be the radius of a circle. The following program computes and displays the area and circumference of the given circle:

```
# circle
#       Input:    A number that is the radius of a circle
#       Output:   The area and circumference of the given circle
#     Formulas:   Area of a circle = pi * radius * radius
#                 Circumference of a circle = pi * 2 * radius

$pi = 3.14159265;
print "Please type the radius of a circle: ";
$radius = <STDIN>;
$area = $pi * $radius * $radius;
$circumference = $pi * 2 * $radius;
print "A circle of radius $radius has an area of $area \n",
      " and a circumference of $circumference \n";
```

Now that we have shown a complete example, we must explain how you can run it or, for that matter, any other Perl program.

2.8 RUNNING PERL PROGRAMS

Perl programs can be compiled and run in several different ways, which vary somewhat among different operating systems. We discuss only one of those ways in this chapter, but it is one that is likely to work under all operating systems on which Perl is run. Note that we use Perl for the language and perl for the Perl compiler/interpreter program.

One way to run Perl programs is to execute the perl system as a command (with the operating system in command-line mode) and include the Perl program file as a parameter. For example, for the program in file circle.pl,

```
% perl circle.pl
```

The % here represents the prompt for the operating system.

Single-statement programs can be run by typing the -e flag and the statement, delimited with single quotes, on the perl command line, as in

```
% perl -e 'print "Is this easy enough? \n";'
```

Note that some non-UNIX implementations of Perl require that the statement following the -e flag be delimited by double quotes.

If you need to run a two- or three-line program and do not want to mess with an editor, you can type perl on the command line, followed by as many lines of Perl as you like, followed by a line with just an end-of-file character on it. For example, examine the following code:

```
% perl
print "Well, ok! \n";
print "This is also easy! \n";
end-of-file character (for example, Control-D for UNIX)
```

Recall from Chapter 1 that Perl programs are not purely interpreted, as is the case with most operating system command languages. Perl programs are first compiled into an intermediate form, which is then interpreted. The perl compilation phase finds the syntax errors in the program before execution begins. Running perl usually results in translation and execution. The execution part can be avoided by including the -c flag in the command line, as in

```
% perl -c circle.pl
```

Another commonly used flag for running perl is -w, which causes the perl compiler to check for a number of common programming errors and to produce warning messages when suspicious code is found in the program. Without this flag set, perl simply ignores many troublesome errors. We strongly recommend that you always run perl with the warnings flag on.

One example of code that leads to a warning, but no error, is

```
$str = "hello";
...
$sum = 3 + $str;
```

In this case, the string is not a representation of a number and the value zero (undef) will be used. Without having -w set, no note would be made of this.

There are a number of other flags that can be set for the perl system. Some of these are discussed later in this book. Information on all of them can be found in the Perl manpage in the perlrun section.

2.9 BITWISE OPERATORS

Our last task in this chapter is to introduce Perl's bitwise operators, which are interesting and occasionally useful, but not so important that they rate space in the earlier parts of this chapter.

Perl has six operators that treat their operands, which are numbers, as bit strings, rather than numbers. These are bitwise logical AND (&), inclusive OR (|), exclusive OR (^), complement (~), left shift (<<), and right shift (>>). The operands of all of these operators are coerced to integer values if necessary before the operation takes place. When floating-point values are coerced to integer values, the value is truncated, rather than rounded. For example, in the expression

```
3.9 << 2
```

the left operand is converted to 3 (11 in binary) and then is shifted left by 2 bits, producing the value 12 (1100 in binary). The shift operations are arithmetic in the sense that, on most machines, right shifts bring copies of the sign bit into the left end of the left operand. This allows the fast shift operators to replace the relatively slow multiplication and division operators when the second operand is a power of 2. For instance, to multiply the value in $x by 8, we could use

```
$x << 3
```

To divide the value in $x by 16, we could use

```
$x >> 4
```

However, the shifts may be machine dependent due to differences in integer representation. Furthermore, unless the operation is going to be done a huge number of times, the increase in execution speed gained by using shifts is negligible.

The bitwise logical and complement operators perform their operations on all of the bits of their operands. Each pair of corresponding bits produces, independently, one bit of the result. For example, if the values of $x and $y are 00010011 and 00110010, respectively, the value of

```
$x | $y
```

is 00110011.

The complement operator (~), which takes just one operand, changes all zeros in its operand to ones, and all ones to zeros.

The &, |, and ^ operators present one of the few cases where you must be concerned about the difference between numbers and strings. If both operands of one of these operators are strings and have not been used as numbers since being assigned, the behavior of the operators is different. Because it is rarely useful, we do not describe this here.

Perl also includes AND and OR operators that are not bitwise, for use with operands that have Boolean values. These are discussed in Chapter 3.

2.10 SUMMARY

Numbers are one of the three scalar types in Perl. They are nearly always stored as double-precision floating-point values. Scalar variable names always begin with a dollar sign, a convention that allows them to be implicitly defined. Such implicitly defined variables are global, meaning they are visible in the whole file in which they appear.

Perl includes the usual numeric operators for multiplication, division, addition, subtraction, and modulus. It also has the increment and decrement operators from C. Perl has typical rules for operator precedence and associativity.

String literals can be delimited by either single quotes or double quotes. The differences between these are that variables that are embedded in those delimited by double quotes are interpolated, and double-quoted strings can include escape sequences to specify special characters. There are two string operators, one for catenation and one for repetition. There are also some string functions, specifically for removing the last character or a trailing input record separator, for the length of the string, for converting alphabetic characters to uppercase or lowercase, for converting hex and octal numbers in strings to numbers, for converting a character to its ASCII numeric code, for searching a string for a particular substring, and for extracting substrings. The `join` operator puts strings together into one new string.

Perl includes a simple assignment operator and compound assignment operators, which combine other binary operators with the assignment operator.

Input can be gotten from the keyboard by specifying the standard input filehandle, `STDIN`, in pointed brackets. Screen output is done with a simple function, `print`, or the more flexible `printf`.

Perl has six bitwise operators, which specify logical AND, inclusive OR, exclusive OR, complement, left shift, and right shift. The operands for all of these are implicitly converted to integers before the operation takes place.

2.11 EXERCISES

Write, test, and debug (if necessary) Perl programs for the following specifications:

1. Input: Two numbers that represent the radius and height of a cylinder, on separate lines, from the keyboard.
   Output: The volume of the cylinder.

2. Input: Four numbers, each on its own line, from the keyboard.
   Output: The sum and average of the numbers.

3. Input: Three lines, each containing a single word, from the keyboard.
   Output: The three input strings, catenated together, but separated with pound signs (#).

4. Input: Two lines, with a string on the first and a number on the second, from the keyboard.
   Output: The input string repeated the number of times specified with the input number, with adjacent instances of the string separated with periods.

5. Input: Three numbers, a, b, and c, each on its own line, from the keyboard.
   Output: The value of the expression
   8ab-(c/4)/17.32
   Method: You must use shift operators for the multiplication and division by powers of 2.

6. Input: A string from the keyboard.
   Output: The input string with all lowercase letters in the first five characters converted to uppercase and all uppercase letters in the second five characters converted to lowercase.

7. Input: A string from the keyboard.
   Output: The input string with the last character (not counting the newline) removed, if it is an `'s'`.

8. Input: A number from the keyboard.

   Output: The input number, with one place right of the decimal point, and again with three places right of the decimal point.

9. Input: Two numbers, each on its own line, from the keyboard.

   Output: The first number, left justified in the first column, and the second number, right justified in column 20.

10. Input: A string of 10 characters from the keyboard.

    Output: The last five characters of the string in columns 1–5 and the first five in columns 6–10.

11. Input: A four-digit number from the keyboard.

    Output: The middle two digits of the input number.

C H A P T E R   3

Control Statements

The collection of control statements in a programming language provides an important part of the character of the language. In this regard, Perl shines, for it includes a wider variety of control statements than virtually any other contemporary language. This chapter describes most of Perl's control statements. It also includes a brief introduction to the Perl debugger, which is an important tool for Perl programmers. Programs written using only the Perl constructs introduced in Chapters 1 and 2 are so simple that their authors should not need a debugger. However, the addition of control statements supports more complex programs, for which that may not always be true.

A fundamental part of most control statements is their control expressions, which are the basis for execution control flow. Therefore, before we consider Perl's control statements, we must describe the form and meaning of its control expressions.

3.1 CONTROL EXPRESSIONS

A control expression must evaluate to values that can be interpreted as true or false. Perl has no Boolean type, which would have just true and false as its range of values, but instead allows scalar expressions to be used to specify control expressions. So, control expressions are always evaluated as either strings or numbers, with the final value being interpreted as either true or false. The control expression of a control statement can be simple, relational, or compound. These three kinds of control expressions are described in the following subsections.

3.1.1 SIMPLE CONTROL EXPRESSIONS

A simple control expression is either an arithmetic expression or a string expression. The value of a simple control expression is interpreted with the following rules: If the value is a string, its value is true, unless it is either the empty string (`" "`) or a zero string (`"0"`). If the value is a number, it is true unless, it is zero. As implied by the other rules, any undefined value is false (because an undefined number is interpreted as zero and an undefined string is interpreted as the empty string). There are some odd cases that can cause confusion. For example, the string literal `"0.0"` looks like zero, but because it is not `"0"`, it is true. All in all, the system is simple and effective—nearly all scalar values evaluate to a Boolean value in the most intuitive way.

3.1.2 RELATIONAL EXPRESSIONS

A relational expression is one that includes a single relational operator, such as >. In Perl, there are two sets of six relational operators, one for numeric operands and one for string operands. All of these operators are shown in Table 3.1.

The relational operators produce `1` for true and the empty string (`" "`) for false. Recall that when the empty string is interpreted as a number, its value is `0`.

The relational operators always coerce their operands to the proper type. For example, in the expression

```
"fruit" eq 7
```

the number `7` will be coerced to `"7"` (because the `eq` operator takes string operands).

The reason there are two sets of relational operators is to avoid certain odd results that could otherwise occur. For example, suppose that we have the expression

```
"27" gt "3"
```

In this expression, the string relational operator `gt` would first compare only the first characters of the two operands (`"2"` and `"3"`). Because the ASCII code for `"2"` comes before the ASCII code for `"3"`, the expression would evaluate to false. However, if the > operator were used, the result would be true, because both operands would be coerced to numbers. So, strings that are known to be numbers can be compared with the numeric operators to get valid results. However, beware of using numeric operators between strings that may *not* be numbers. For instance,

```
"boy" == "girl"
```

Table 3.1

PERL'S RELATIONAL OPERATORS

Operation	Numeric	String
Is equal to	==	eq
Is not equal to	!=	ne
Is less than	<	lt
Is greater than	>	gt
Is less than or equal to	<=	le
Is greater than or equal to	>=	ge

is always true, as neither operand is a number and both are coerced to zero, the numeric value of `undef`.

The precedence of the "equal to" relational operators, `==`, `!=`, `eq`, and `ne` is lower than that of the "nonequal to" operators, `<`, `<=`, `>`, `>=`, `lt`, `le`, `gt`, and `ge`. All of these have precedence lower than that of the arithmetic operators. So, when arithmetic expressions are used as the operands of a relational operator, they need not be parenthesized to ensure that they are evaluated before the relational operator. For example, in

```
0.03 * $a < $limit
```

the comparison is done after the multiplication. However, for the sake of readability, we recommend the use of the parentheses to clarify the evaluation order of such expressions. So, we prefer the preceding expression to appear as

```
(0.03 * $a) < $limit
```

Because the value of a relational expression is a scalar, it can be stored in a scalar variable, as in

```
$over_limit = ($spent > 10_000);
```

Once again, the relational expression is parenthesized only to enhance the readability of the statement.

The relational operators are nonassociative, which makes

```
$a > $b > $c
```

syntactically invalid. Perl has two operators that are sometimes discussed with the relational operators, the comparison operators, `<=>` and `cmp`. These are discussed in Chapter 6. The third kind of control expression, a compound expression, is the most complicated.

3.1.3 COMPOUND EXPRESSIONS

Compound expressions consist of scalar variables, scalar literals, relational expressions, and Boolean operators. A compound expression could have any number of Boolean operators. Perl has two sets of Boolean operators with the same semantics, but different precedence levels. One set is borrowed from C. These are `&&` for AND, `||` for OR, and `!` for NOT. The precedence of these operators is lower than that of the relational operators.

The `&&` and `||` operators are short-circuit operators, which means that only the left operand is evaluated if its value determines the value of the expression. If the Boolean operator is `&&`, this means that if the left operand evaluates to false, the right operand is not evaluated. For example, in

```
($a > 0) && ($b < $limit)
```

if `$a` is not greater than zero, the second comparison (between `$b` and `$limit`) is not done. This is only significant when the second operand of the Boolean operator is an expression that has the side effect of changing the value of some variable. For instance, consider

```
($a > 0) && (++$b < $limit)
```

If `$a` is not greater than zero, the value of `$b` will not be affected by the evaluation of this expression.

For the Boolean operator ||, if the left operand evaluates to be true, the right operand is not evaluated. The value produced by the && and || operators is the last value evaluated, rather than true or false (1 or " "). For example, in

```
$a && $b
```

if $a is 17 and $b is 9, which makes the value of the expression true, the actual value of the expression is 9, rather than 1.

The operators denoted by and, or, and not are exactly like the &&, ||, and ! operators, except that they are more readable and have lower precedence. In fact, their precedence is lower than that of any other Perl operators. This means that no matter what kind of expressions (except other Boolean expressions) are used as their operands, these Boolean operators will always be evaluated last.

All of the binary Boolean operators (but not the relational operators) can be compounded with the assignment operator, as in

```
$a ||= $b;
```

This statement performs the OR operation between $a and $b and puts the result in $a.

The precedence and associativity of all of the operators discussed up to now is shown in Table 3.2. The operators at the top have the highest precedence.

The value of a Boolean expression formed with and and or, as is the case with && and ||, is the last value evaluated, rather than 1 or " ".

We are now ready to begin discussing the control statements of Perl. We begin with the selection statements (which include if and unless) and conditional expressions.

Table 3.2

OPERATOR PRECEDENCE AND ASSOCIATIVITY

Operators	Associativity
++ --	nonassociative
**	right
~ ! unary + and –	right
* / % x	left
+ – .	left
<< >>	left
> < >= <= lt gt le ge	nonassociative
== != eq ne	nonassociative
&	left
| ^	left
&&	left
||	left
= += -= *= **= /= &= <<= >>= &&= |= ||= .= %= ^= x=	right
not	right
and	left
or xor	left

The statements whose execution is controlled with a Perl control statement are specified with a block. A Perl block, which could contain a single statement, is delimited by braces ({}). A *control construct* is a control statement and the block whose execution it controls.

3.2 SELECTION STATEMENTS—if AND unless

A selection statement is used to choose between two alternative paths of execution. As is the case with most other programming languages, Perl's primary selection statement is named if. A Perl if construct can include two blocks, one executed if the control expression is true—called the *then clause*—and one executed if the control expression is false—called the *else clause*. The else clause may be omitted.

The syntax of Perl's if statement with an else is

```
if (control expression) {
    # then clause statements
} else {
    # else clause statements
}
```

Following is an example of an if statement without an else clause:

```
if ($a > $b) {
    print "\$a is greater than \$b \n";
    $max = $a;
}
```

An example of an if with an else clause is

```
# Recall that zero is interpreted as false
if ($total) {
    $average = $sum / $total;
    print "The average is $average \n";
} else {
    print "The average cannot be computed--the total is zero \n";
}
```

Notice that we indented the statements in the then clause by four spaces and aligned the right brace under the beginning of if. These are the common Perl style conventions that are used throughout the book. They make the statement flow structure of the if construct obvious to all readers. It is a common practice among Perl users that when a block has just one statement and it is short, the block can be on the line with if. However, we believe that Perl programs are more readable if all blocks are consistent in form, always having the block's statements on their own lines. Therefore, we prefer

```
if ($a > $b) {
    print "Largest: $a \n";
}
```

over

```
if ($a > $b) { print "Largest: $a \n"; }
```

The last statement in a multistatement block need not end with a semicolon, but it is a good practice, in case a statement is added later after the last statement in the block.

In some situations, it is convenient for a selection statement to have an else clause, but no then clause. You could, of course, reverse the logic of the control expression and put what was the else clause in the then clause. However, such statements are sometimes confusing, because of the inverted control expression. Perl has an alternative, unless, that does not require the logic reversal. For example, examine the following statement:

```
unless (($count < $limit) or $nolimit) {
    print "I simply cannot go on! \n"
}
```

In this construct, the print is executed only if $count is greater than or equal to $limit, and $nolimit is zero.

An if statement that appears in the then clause or else clause of another if statement is called a *nested* if statement. Nested if statements quickly become difficult to read as their depth increases beyond two. A common convention for this problem is always to make the nested if the else clause, rather than the then clause.[1] Such constructs are easier to understand than those in which the nested if statement is in the then clause. Perl includes a special word for building nested if constructs in which the nested one is in the else clause, elsif (not elseif). Consider the following construct:

```
if ($age < 18) {
    print "You're just a kid! \n";
} elsif ($age < 40) {
    print "Not a kid, but still young \n";
} elsif ($age < 65) {
    print "Middle aged, huh? \n";
} else {
    print "You're now in the 'Golden Age', right? \n";
}
```

Perl does not include a switch or case statement for coding multiple selection constructs. However, it is easy to build similar constructs in Perl, as you will see in Section 3.4.

Perl includes a construct that implements a simple form of selection structure, called a conditional expression. A conditional expression chooses one of two expressions to be evaluated and has the form
Boolean_expression ? then_expression : else_expression

Conditional expressions are commonly used as the right side of assignment statements, as in

---

[1]This builds a construct in which the controlled clauses are in effect connected by OR operators. Nesting an if statement in a then clause builds a construct in which the controlled clauses are in effect connected by AND operators.

```
$average = ($number != 0)? $sum / $number : 0;
```

If both the then and else expressions have l-values, the conditional expression can be used as the left side of an assignment statement, as in

```
(($next > 0) ? $positives : $negatives) += next;
```

The example that follows illustrates Perl's `if` statement. It reads three unique numbers from the keyboard, determines which is numerically in the middle, and displays that number. The strategy is to use nested `if` statements with compound control expressions first to determine whether the first number has the middle value, and then to determine the same with the second number. If both of these tests fail, the program correctly assumes that the third number has the middle value.

```
# middle
#    Input:   Three  unique  numbers,  on  separate  lines,  from  the
keyboard
#    Output:  The input number whose value is smaller than the largest
and
#                larger than the smallest
# Get the input numbers

$first = <STDIN>;
$second = <STDIN>;
$third = <STDIN>;

# Is the first number the middle one?

if ((($first < $second) and ($first > $third)) or
    (($first < $third) and ($first > $second))) {
    $middle = $first;

# Is the second number the middle one?

} elsif ((($second < $first) and ($second > $third)) or
        (($second < $third) and ($second > $first))) {
    $middle = $second;
}

# It must be the third one

else {
    $middle = $third
}

print "The middle input number is: $middle \n";
```

Next, we discuss Perl statements for building iterative constructs.

3.3 ITERATIVE STATEMENTS—while, until, AND for

Perl has several statements for specifying iterative constructs, or loops. The ability to control the repetitive execution of statement collections is a fundamental source of the power of computers. Iterative statements are therefore essential in all programming languages. As is the case with other programming languages, Perl includes iterative statements in which the repetition control is a Boolean expression (`while` and `until`)—and one in which the control is based on a counter (`for`). Perl also includes a third kind of loop statement, `foreach`, in which iteration is controlled by the number of elements in the given array. This section describes all of these, except `foreach`, which is described in conjunction with the discussion of arrays in Chapter 4. The following subsection discusses the simplest and most general iterative statements, those that use Boolean expressions for control.

3.3.1   `while` **AND** `until` **LOOPS**

A `while` statement has the form

```
while (control expression) {
    # loop body
}
```

When a `while` statement is executed, its control expression is evaluated and, if true, the loop body is executed. Then the control expression is evaluated again, and so forth until it evaluates to false. Because the control mechanism is executed and affects statement execution flow before the loop body is executed, `while` loops are called *pretest* loops. As an example of a `while` loop, consider

```
$sum = 0;

while ($sum <= 1000) {
    $sum += <STDIN>;
    ...
}
```

The `until` statement is similar to `while`, except that the value of the control expression is used in the opposite way. For example, examine this code:

```
$sum = 0;

until ($sum > 1000) {
    $sum += <STDIN>;
    ...
}
```

Loops formed with `until`, like those formed with `while`, are pretest loops.

3.3.2   **THE** `for` **STATEMENT**

In many situations, because the number of iterations of a loop is known when the loop execution begins, it is convenient to use a loop controlled by a counter. The `for` statement is designed for building loops whose control depends on a counter. Its general form is

```
for (initial expression; control expression; increment expression) {
    # loop body
}
```

The initial and increment expressions are usually either assignment statements or expressions with side effects, for example, $count++. The semantics of for are easiest to explain in terms of a while statement. The general for statement has the same effect as the following code:

```
initial expression;
while (control expression) {
      # loop body
    increment expression;
}
```

This code shows that for, like while, specifies a pretest loop. The following code gets 10 numbers from the keyboard and computes their sum:

```
$sum = 0;

for ($count = 0; $count < 10; $count++) {
    $value = <STDIN>;
    $sum += $value;
}
```

All three expressions in a for statement are optional, but the semicolons are not. If the control expression is omitted, it is interpreted as true, making the loop what is often called an *infinite loop*. An infinite loop is an iterative construct in which the control mechanism has a fixed value that never causes the loop to complete its execution. Such loops usually include a statement in their bodies that provides an escape from the loop.

All three expressions in a for statement can be multiple expressions or statements, separated by commas. The comma is an operator in this case. The value returned by a list of comma-separated expressions and/or statements is that of the last. For example, the value of $x after execution of the statement

```
$x = ($a = 7, $b = 10, $c = -2);
```

is -2. Note that the expression

```
$a = 7, $b = 10, $c = -2;
```

by itself is valid in Perl.

The comma-separated expressions in a for statement are most often used to allow more than one variable to be initialized or incremented in a for statement.[2] In this respect, consider the code:

```
for ($forward = 0, $backward = 10;
    $forward < 10;
    $forward++, $backward--) {
    ...
}
```

---

[2] If we want two statements in the initial expression, we cannot use a semicolon to separate them, because it would be interpreted as specifying the end of the initial expression.

Assignment statements are sometimes used for the control expression in a `for` statement. Consider the following loop:

```
for ($sum = 0; $value = <STDIN>; $sum += $value) {}
```

This loop is a generalization of the earlier loop that inputs data and computes their sum. In this case, the loop reads input data from the keyboard until EOF is typed. Recall that the value of an assignment statement is the value that was assigned. When `<STDIN>` gets EOF, it returns the empty string, which represents false. Getting an empty line does not return false, because such a line still has the newline character(s). Of course, a `chomp`ed empty line is an empty string, so it will represent false. However, in the preceding example, which does not use `chomp`, the loop continues for any input except EOF.

We could use the same control expression in a `while` statement, as in

```
$sum = 0;

while ($value = <STDIN>) {
    $sum += $value;
}
```

There are no restrictions on what can be in the body of a `for` loop. In particular, any variable that appears in the expressions of the `for` can be changed in the loop body, although that is not usually a good idea, because such changes make the loop more difficult to understand.

Not all loops can be simply and conveniently modeled with `while`, `unless`, or `for`. The following section describes additional Perl statements for building these more complex loops.

3.4   WAYS OUT OF A BLOCK—`next`, `last`, AND `redo`

Perl provides several control operators, `last`, `next`, and `redo`, that can appear in blocks and provide abnormal statement flow control. Most often, these operators are used in the bodies of loops, but they can be used in any block.

When the `next` operator appears without an operand in a block, its execution transfers control to the end of that block. If the block in which `next` appears is a `while`, `until`, or `for`, control goes back to the control expression of the loop. Consider the following code:

```
while (substr($next_line = <STDIN>, 0, 1) ne "~") {
    if (length($next_line) < 5) {
        next;
    }
    $first4 = substr($next_line, 0, 4);
    if ($first4 eq "jack") {
        $count++;
    }
}
```

In this code, a new string is gotten from the keyboard in each iteration. The loop terminates when a new string begins with `"~"`. If a line has fewer than five characters (meaning that it cannot include `"jack"` and the newline), the remainder of the iteration is skipped. If a line begins with `"jack"`, $count is incremented. This is one of those somewhat rare instances where an input string need not be immediately chomped. A `last` operator that appears in a loop body and is executed causes the loop to be immediately terminated. Control is transferred to the first statement after the loop body.

A `redo` operator that appears in a loop body and is executed causes transfer of control to the top of the loop body (not the control expression). The iteration is simply redone, without reevaluating the control expression. Replacing the `next` in the earlier loop with `redo` would be a bad idea, for it would result in an infinite loop.

The `last`, `next`, and `redo` control operators are often used in conjunction with labeled blocks. The form of a label is an identifier, followed by a colon, as in

```
LOOP:
   while (…) {
   }   …
```

If a loop is nested inside another loop, `next`, `last`, and `redo` operators that do not have operands affect only the loop in which they appear (rather than any enclosing loops). Sometimes it is convenient for these operators to affect some enclosing loop. This is the purpose of placing a label on a loop. If a loop has a label and that label is the operand of a `next`, `last`, or `redo` operator that appears in a nested loop, these operators affect the labeled loop, rather than the smallest one in which the operator appears. For example, consider the following code:

```
OUTER:
   for ($out_index = 100; $out_index < 1000; $out_index += 100) {
      for ($in_index = 100; $in_index < 1000; $in_index += 100){
         $product = $in_index * $out_index;
         if ($product > 872e3) {
            last OUTER;
         } else {
            print "Next product is $product \n";
         }
      }
   }
```

When the `if` control expression evaluates to true, the loop labeled OUTER is terminated.

Bare blocks (those that are not part of a loop construct) can be labeled and can include `last`, `next`, or `redo` operators. The `last` operator can be used to build a multiple selection construct, as in

```
SWITCH: {
   if ($word eq "bob") {
      $bob++;
      last SWITCH;
   }
   if ($word eq "darcie") {
      $darcie++;
      last SWITCH;
```

```
        }
        if ($word eq "jake") {
            $jake++;
            last SWITCH;
        }
        $nobody++;
    }
```

Perl includes a special block called a `continue` block, which can follow any other block. `continue` blocks interact with the `next` operator, if it happens to appear in the preceding block. Because of their relatively rare use, we will not discuss the purpose and use of `continue` blocks.

3.5   STATEMENT MODIFIERS

In some situations, we need to select or repeat the execution of a single statement, rather than a block. Single statements and `do` blocks can be followed by a modifier to control their execution. We will explain `do` blocks shortly. The possible modifiers are

>`if` expression,
>`unless` expression,
>`while` expression,
>`until` expression,

and

>`foreach` expression. (See Chapter 5.)

Notice that the control expressions in statement modifiers are not parenthesized, as they are in the corresponding control statements. When these modifiers follow single statements, their semantics are almost as you would expect. For instance, consider this:

```
$bob++ if $word eq "bob";
$sum *= 2 until $sum > 1000;
```

One somewhat surprising aspect of these modifiers is that even though the control expression is at the end of the statement, it is evaluated first. Neither the `while` nor the `until` modifiers build posttest loops (loops with the test performed after each iteration).

A `do` block is a bare block that is preceded by `do`, as in

```
do {
    chomp($word = <STDIN>);
    $bob++ if $word eq "bob";
}
```

In this form, the `do` does nothing. However, a `do` block can be followed by a modifier, as in

```
chomp($word = <STDIN>);
do {
```

```
        $bob++ if $word eq "bob";
        chomp($word = <STDIN>);
    } until $word eq "~";
```

When a `while` or `until` is the modifier on a `do` block, the construct is a posttest loop. The control expression is evaluated *after* the block is executed, rather than before, as is the case in normal `while` and `until` constructs and in single statements modified by `while` or `until`. So, the `while` and `until` statements and single-statement modifiers are pretest, but when used to modify a `do` block, they are posttest. Consider the following example:

```
$sum = 1;
while ($sum < 1) {
    $sum *= 2;
}
$sum = 1;
$sum *= 2 until $sum < 1;
$sum = 1;
do {
    $sum *= 2;
} while $sum < 1;
```

The first two of these leave the value of $sum at 1. The last one changes it to 2, because the `do` block is executed once before the control expression is evaluated.

Statement modifiers should be used only if you think a program reader (including yourself) would find the statement more important than the control expression.

There are situations that can arise during program execution in which you simply want the program to print a message and quit. This is conveniently done in Perl with the `die` function, which is described in the following section.

3.6   STOPPING EXECUTION WITH die

The `die` function takes a list of parameters. When called, it catenates its parameters together, prints them on STDERR, and terminates program execution. STDERR is a standard output filehandle whose output usually ends up in the same place as STDOUT. Typically, `die` has a single string literal parameter, as in

```
die "The input file is empty!"
```

When a `die` function is executed, the Perl system catenates some information to the end of its parameter string. This usually includes the program name, the line number of the `die`, and a newline. If the newline is included, this information is not provided. Because of this, the string parameter of `die` often does not include a newline.

In many situations, `die` is called when a system function has failed. The number of the system error is stored in $!. Therefore, in many cases $! is included in the string parameter to `die`. For example, consider the statement

```
die "Input/output function error $!";
```

If you want the program to terminate without providing any information, you can use the `exit` function, which takes a numeric parameter as an error number. The error number 0 means normal termination, as in

```
exit 0
```

Now that we have discussed most of Perl's control statements and statement modifiers, we can expand on the descriptions of input operations that were presented in Chapter 2.

3.7   A BIT MORE ABOUT INPUT

In the following two subsections, we discuss how line input operators can be used for control expressions and how command-line arguments can specify the names of input files.

3.7.1   LINE INPUT OPERATORS IN CONTROL EXPRESSIONS

The line input operator can be used in the control expression of a `while` statement. When it is the whole control expression, the value gotten from standard input is assigned to the implicit variable, $_ which is the target of the line input operator *only* as the control expression of a `while` statement, a `for` statement, or a `while` statement modifier. As an example, consider the following:

```
while (<STDIN>) {
    print;
    chomp;
    if ($_ eq "money") {
        print "I've finally found it!!! \n";
    }
}
```

The default use of $_ occurs in three places in this code: as the target of the implicit assignment of the input line from <STDIN>, as the operand of the `print` operator, and as the operand of the `chomp` operator.

The $_ variable should be used only as a temporary variable. It should never be used over more than a few lines of code, because it is frequently used by different operators and functions. One advantage of implicit variables, especially $_, is that they save inventing and typing many variable names in a program. Novice Perl programmers sometimes consider Perl's use of $_ to be magic and mysterious, but it is really just a practicality.

3.7.2   COMMAND-LINE ARGUMENTS

It has long been a common practice in UNIX programming to use a command-line argument to specify an input file for a program. This technique can be used in Perl programs, regardless of the computer on which they are run. A command-line argument is a string that appears after the rest of a command that executes a program, as in

```
% perl maximum.pl salaries.dat
```

In this case, the command is to run `perl` on the Perl program file `maximum.pl`, specifying the argument `salaries.dat`. While it is often the case that a command-line argument is a file name that specifies input to the program, it could also specify a destination for output from it. Because there is no syntactic difference between the specification of an input file and that of an output file, `salaries.dat` in the preceding example could be either. The reason for specifying a data input file this way is to allow the program to be used on different input files. Without this mechanism, one would need to modify the program between uses or to read the name of the input file from the keyboard.

In Perl, command-line arguments are implicitly redirected to a special filehandle that is the default for the line input operator. So, the input line operator `<>` reads lines from the file specified on the command line. The following loop reads input lines from the file specified on the command line and prints them:

```
while (<>) {
    print;
}
```

Once again, the special variable `$_` is being used as the target of the implicit assignment in the control expression and as the operand of `print`.

If more than one command-line argument is specified, the files are read one at a time until the EOF in the last file is read. If no command-line argument is specified, the empty `<>` gets lines from standard input (the keyboard).

Command-line arguments are directly accessible in Perl, so they can be used for much more than simply supplying input file names. This is discussed in Chapter 4. (Command-line file specification also works when Perl is run from a DOS command line.)

3.8   AN EXAMPLE

The program that follows reads a list of numbers from the file specified as a command-line argument and finds and prints the second smallest number in the list, along with its position in the list. Of course, its real purpose is to illustrate some of the Perl control statements.

```
# small
#    Input:   A text file containing one number per line, where
#             the file is taken from the command line
#    Output:  The second smallest number in the file, along with
#             its position in the file, with 1 being the position
#             of the first number

# Get the first two numbers and initialize the smallest, its
#   position, the second smallest, and its position
# If there are fewer than two numbers, print a message and die

if ($first = <>) {
    if ($second = <>) {
        if ($first < $second) {
            $min = $first;
            $pos_min = 1;
            $second_min = $second;
            $pos_2nd_min = 2;
```

```
            } else {
                $min = $second;
                $pos_min = 2;
                $second_min = $first;
                $pos_2nd_min = 1;
            }
        } else {
            "The file has only one line!";
        }
    } else {
        die "The file is empty!";
    }

$position = 2;

# Loop to read and process the rest of the file

while ($next = <>) {
        $position++;

# If the new number is the new smallest, replace both the
#   smallest and the second smallest

        if ($next < $min) {
            $second_min = $min;
            $min = $next;
            $pos_2nd_min = $pos_min;
            $pos_min = $position;

# If the new number is between the smallest and the second
#   smallest, replace the second smallest with the new number

        } elsif ($next > $min and $next < $second_min) {
            $second_min = $next;
            $pos_2nd_min = $position;
        }
    }

print "The second smallest number is: $second_min \n";
print "The position of the second smallest is: $pos_2nd_min \n";
```

The strategy in this program is as follows: First, it gets the first two numbers from the input file and initializes the values of the variables that store smallest and second smallest numbers in the file, along with the variables that store their positions in the file. It then reads the remainder of the file, one number at a time. Any new number could be either the new smallest number or the new second smallest number in the file. So, for each new number the program must determine whether it must become the new value of the variable that stores the smallest or second smallest in the file. Every time a variable that stores the smallest or second smallest is changed, the variable that stores the position of the changed variable must also be updated.

3.9 THE DEBUGGER

One of the important tools for a programmer is a debugger. The `perl` system has a debugger that includes many of the usual debugger features. When the -d switch is set on the command line that executes `perl`, the program runs under the control of the debugger.[3] For example, if we run the program of Section 3.8, `small`, with the -d switch set, `perl` responds with

```
Loading DB routines from perl5db.pl version 1.0401
Emacs support available.

Enter h or `h h' for help.

main::(small:12):                  if ($first = <>) {
  DB<1>
```

The debugger sets up for execution, but does not actually execute any code. The second to last line of the example indicates that the next line to be executed, which is the first executable line of the program, is in program `small`, line 12. The source code on line 12 also appears on the line. The last line (DB<1>) is the debugger prompt, which invites the user to provide debugger commands.

The command |h causes the debugger help file to be displayed, one window full at a time. Typing h, followed by some command, produces the help information for the specified command. The most commonly used debugger operations are to control execution, display the values of program variables, display part of the source program, and change the values of program variables. The execution of a single line of a program is requested with the s command—for example

```
DB<1>s
```

In our example, this would result in

```
main::(small:13)                       if ($second = <>) {
```

The n command requests execution to the next line, but ignores any subprogram that is called by the executed code. The f command requests execution to proceed to the end of the currently executing subprogram.

A *breakpoint* is a place in a program where the user wants execution to pause. They are set to allow the user to examine the values of variables and perhaps change one or more of those values. In Perl, a breakpoint can be set on any executable statement or the first line of a subprogram with the b command. For example,

```
DB<1>b 17
```

sets a breakpoint just before line 17. The command

```
DB<11>b fixer
```

sets a breakpoint just before the first executable line of the subprogram `fixer`. The c command requests execution from the current position in the program until just before the next breakpoint. For instance, in our program, if we set a breakpoint at line 39 and use c, we would get

---

[3]Actually, the -d switch causes the compiler to insert Perl code into the program. This code allows the interpreter to executes the program as if it were being executed under the control of a typical debugging system.

```
DB<1> b 39
DB<2> c
main::(small:39):                while ($next = <>) {
```

If a line number is included in a c command, a temporary breakpoint is set at the specified line number, and the program is executed to just before that line. For example, the command

```
DB<1> c 39
```

has the same effect as the just-discussed b and c commands.

Both b commands (the one for line numbers and the one for subprogram names) can include a Boolean expression in brackets. This means that the breakpoint is effective only when the Boolean expression is true. For instance, consider the following command:

```
DB<1)> b 39 [$pos_min == 2]
```

The L command lists all lines that have breakpoints set.

A breakpoint on a specific line can be deleted with the d command. For example, to get rid of a breakpoint at line 39, we would use

```
DB<2> d 39
```

The D command deletes all breakpoints in the program.

You often need to look at parts of the program you are working on during the debugging process. The w command takes a line number as a parameter and displays a few lines on either side of the specified line number. For example,

```
DB<3> w 44
```

displays

```
41
42  # If the new number is the new smallest, replace both the
43  #   smallest and the second smallest
44
45:      if ($next < $min) {
46:          $second_min = $min;
47:          $min = $next;
48:          $pos_2nd_min = $pos_min;
49:          $pos_min = $position;
50      }
```

The command

```
p expression
```

evaluates the given expression and displays its value. This is normally used to display the current values of program and implicit variables at a breakpoint.

The x command takes a Perl expression as its parameter. It interprets the expression in list context and displays the result. For example, consider the following commands on our example program:

```
main::(small:12)              if ($first = <>) {
  DB<1> b 39
  DB<2> c
main::(small:39)              while ($next = <>) {
  DB<3> p $first
```

```
   1
   DB<4> x $first = 2
 0   2
   DB<5> p $first
 2
```

The x command allows you to change the values of any variables in your program, including the implicit variables. This is useful for forcing execution along specific control paths of the program during testing or debugging.

Execution of a program can be "traced," which means that every source line that is executed is listed, along with its line number, when it is executed. For example, if we set a breakpoint at line 35, set the trace toggle switch to "on" by typing the t command, and then using the c command, we get

```
main::(small:12)              if ($first = <>) {
   DB<1> b 39
   DB<2> t
Trace = on
   DB<2> c
main::(small:13)                  if ($second = <>) {
main::(small:14)                      if ($first < $second) {
main::(small:21)                          $min = $second;
main::(small:22)                          $pos_min = 2;
main::(small:23)                          $second_min = $first;
main::(small:24)                          $pos_2nd_min = 1;
main::(small:35)                  $position = 2;
main::(small:39)              while ($next = <>) {
   DB<2>
```

The trace can be turned off by another use of the t command.

Finally, the q command terminates the interpretation of the program.

Table 3.3 lists the debugger commands described in this section.

Table 3.3

A SUMMARY OF DEBUGGER COMMANDS

Command	Action
s	Executes one line.
n	Executes the next line.
f	Executes to the end of the subprogram.
b k	Sets a breakpoint at line k.
b subx	Sets a breakpoint at the beginning of function subx.
c	Executes to the next breakpoint.
c k	Executes to line k.
L	Lists all breakpoints.
d k	Deletes the breakpoint at line k.
w k	Displays lines around line k.
p expr	Evaluates expr and display the result.
x expr	Evaluates expr in list context and display the result.
t	Switch traces mode on (or off).
q	Terminates the program.

3.10 SUMMARY

Perl has the usual collection of control statements, but also includes some not-so-usual statement modifiers and control operators. Control expressions always evaluate to either strings or numbers. The empty string and the string consisting of just a zero represent false; all other strings represent true. The numeric value zero represents false, while all other numbers represent true.

Perl has two sets of relational operators, one for numbers and one for strings. These operators can cause coercions of their operands. The comparison operators (`<=>` for numbers and `cmp` for strings) return 1, 0, or -1, rather than 1 or `""`. Perl includes the C logical operators `&&`, `||`, and `!`, and a new set of more readable low-precedence operators `and`, `or`, and `not`.

All Perl compound statements, which are delimited with braces, can be blocks (meaning that they can define local variables). All control statements control blocks, so the controlled statements must always be delimited by braces, even when there is only a single statement inside. Perl has a reverse logic form of `if` (named `unless`) and a reverse logic form of `while` (named `until`). Both `while` and `until` form pretest loops. The `for` statement is a powerful and flexible loop control statement, usually used for counting loops.

Perl has three control operators that are usually used in loop bodies. These are `next` (which forces control to the end of the loop body), `last` (which forces control out of the loop construct), and `redo` (which causes the current iteration to be repeated). These three operators can include a loop label as an operand to specify that their action is to be taken on the named enclosing loop, rather than the smallest loop in which they appear.

There are five statement modifiers that can be attached to the end of single statements: `if`, `unless`, `while`, `until`, and `foreach`. In all of these cases, the modifier is executed first. However, when attached to a `do` block, they are executed after the `do` block is executed.

The `die` function is used to print a message and kill execution of the program. The `exit` function can be used for the same purpose when no message is useful.

The line input operator (pointed or angle brackets) can appear as the right side of an assignment that serves as the control expression in `while` and `for` statements. When it does, it is only false when the EOF character is returned by the input operator. When the line input operator is the whole control expression, the implicit variable `$_` is used. This variable is also the default operand of `print` and `chomp` (and many other functions, some of which are discussed later in the book).

If an empty line input operator (`<>`) appears as the whole control expression in a `while` or `for` statement, the lines are obtained from the file or files that were specified in the command line that ran the program. If no command line arguments were included, the lines are gotten from `STDIN` (the keyboard).

The Perl debugger offers capabilities that are similar to those provided by other common debugger systems. A debugger is a powerful tool for understanding how or why programs do or do not operate correctly.

3.11 EXERCISES

Write, test, and debug (if necessary) Perl programs for the following specifications:.

1. Input: A file that contains one name per line, specified on the command line, and one name from the keyboard.

Output: The number of times the name from the keyboard appears in the file.

2. Input: A file that contains one number per line, specified on the command line.

Output: a.   The percentage of numbers in the file that are greater than 0 and less than 50.

b.   The average of the numbers in the file that are less than, 0 or greater than or equal to, 100.

3. Input: A number from the keyboard.

Output: The factorial of the input number, if the number is $> = 0$. For $n > 0$, factorial(n) is $n * (n - 1) * \ldots * 1$. The factorial of 0 is 1. If the input number is less than 0, a message is to be displayed indicating that condition.

4. Input: Three numbers, on separate lines, from the keyboard.

Output: The largest and smallest among the three numbers.

5. Input: Three names, on separate lines, from the keyboard.

Output: The input names, in alphabetical order.

6. Input: Two files of numbers, one per line, specified on the command line.

Output: The average of the first k numbers in the input, where the sum of the first $(k - 1)$st numbers is less than 10,000.

Method: You must use an `until` statement and the input numbers must be read into the implicit variable `$_`.

7. Input: A file in which each line contains a word, specified on the command line.

Output: Each word from the input with its uppercase letters converted to lowercase and its characters in reverse order (without using the `reverse` function).

8. Input: A file of lines of text, specified on the command line.

Output: a.   For every line, the line's length.

b.   For every line that contains the string `"son"`, the line, followed by its length.

9. Input: A file of lines of text, specified on the command line.

Output: Every input line that has more than 10 characters, not counting the newline, but fewer than 20 characters, not counting the newline, that contains the string `"ed"`.

10. Input: A file, specified on the command line, in which each line has a name in the format: positions 1–10 have a first name; positions 20–35 have the last name.

Output: The whole name of the person in the file whose last name belongs first alphabetically among the last names in the file.

CHAPTER 4

Arrays

There are three data types in Perl: scalars, arrays, and associative arrays, or hashes. Chapter 2 discussed scalars; this chapter discusses arrays; Chapter 5 discusses hashes.

Virtually all programming languages support arrays. However, Perl's arrays are far more flexible than those of other common programming languages. This increased flexibility is a result of the late binding of arrays to their attributes. Simply put, Perl arrays more easily bend to the needs of the program. They grow in length as needed, implicitly. They also can be made to shrink during program execution. The types of their elements are also not set in stone at any time. These characteristics amount to a loosening of the limits and restrictions on their use, which makes them easy to use. Furthermore, Perl provides a collection of functions and operators for many of the most common manipulations of arrays and their elements.

4.1   INTRODUCTION TO ARRAYS

Arrays are linear data structures whose elements are referenced through subscripted variables. Perl arrays store lists of scalar values. Recall that a scalar value can be a string, a number, or a reference. Arrays have no type, other than array. An array can contain all numbers, all strings, all references, or any combination of those three kinds of values.

Perl arrays are not defined to have any particular size. They can be empty or they can occupy all of the available memory on your machine. They implicitly grow as needed and can be made to shrink at any time. The lack of a specific element type and the lack of size restrictions make Perl arrays more flexible and powerful than those of most programming languages—another result of the "no unnecessary limits" design philosophy of Perl.

Before we present any further discussion of arrays, we must examine lists and list literals, which serve as array literals.

4.2 LIST LITERALS

A *list* is an ordered sequence of scalar values. A *list literal* is the specification of a list in a program. List literals are usually delimited with parentheses.[1] The simplest list literals are lists of scalar literals, separated by commas and delimited with parentheses. List literal elements can also be scalar variables and expressions. As an example, consider the following:

List literal	*Description*
(5)	a list of one number.
()	The empty list.
("apples", "pcs")	A list of two strings.
("me", 100, "you", 50)	A list of two strings and two numbers.
($sum, "Sum")	A list with one element specified with a variable.
(2 * $total, "!" x 20)	A list with values specified with expressions.
qw(bob carol ted arf)	A list whose elements are implicitly quoted.

A *range operator* (an ellipsis (..)) can be used to specify a range of scalar literals in a list literal. For example, consider the following equivalencies:

List literal	*Equivalent list*
(0 .. 6)	(0, 1, 2, 3, 4, 5, 6)
(1.5 .. 7)	(1.5, 2.5, 3.5, 4.5, 5.5, 6.5)
(5 .. 3)	()

Notice that in the middle example the stepsize between values is 1, even though the first element does not have an integral value. The stepsize is always 1 in list literals.

The range operator also works for string elements, as in

('a' .. 'z')

It even works for strings with multiple characters, as in

('aa' .. 'zz')

which produces a list with 676 elements ('aa', 'ab', 'ac', …).

---

[1]A list literal need not be delimited with parentheses if its context allows it to be clearly identified as a list without parentheses.

The range operator can be used in scalar context, where it behaves quite differently. This is rarely used and is not discussed here. We are now ready to discuss array variables.

4.3 ARRAYS

An *array* is a variable whose value is a list. Names of array variables begin with @, which puts them in a namespace that is distinct from the namespace for scalars. There is no connection between the variables $list and @list. Like scalar variables, array variables need not be declared. Because an array stores a list, its elements are always scalar; its length is whatever is necessary to hold the list that has been assigned to it. An uninitialized array has the empty list as its value; that is, it has the value ().

If an assignment statement has an array variable (without a subscript) as its left side, or target, an array is assigned as a unit, regardless of the form of the right-side expression (although it is most commonly an array or list literal). If the right-side array or list literal of the assignment has more elements than the target array, the target array is stretched to the size of the right-side array or list. If the target array has more elements than the right side, its surplus elements are set to undef. If a scalar value is assigned to an array, the array is set to a single element with that value. Consider the following examples of array assignments:

```
@a = (2, 4, 6);          # @a has three elements
@a = ('a', 'b', 'c', 'x');   # Now @a has four elements
@a = (4.37625);          # @a still has four elements, but
                         #   the last three are undef
@a = 1;                  # @a is (1)
```

If an array is assigned to a scalar variable, the array's length is assigned to the target. For example, in

```
@names = ("mary", "jo", "ann");
$girls = @names;
```

$girls is set to 3.

Array assignments can be parts of expressions. A simple example is

```
@friends = @girl_friends = ("Peggy Sue", "Mary Lou", "Pompadou");
```

A list literal that contains no expressions or literals, that is, it has only variables, can be used as the target of an array assignment. For an example, consider the following statement:

```
($a, $b) = (2, 4);
```

This statement assigns 2 to $a and 4 to $b. If there are fewer variables in the target list than there are elements in the right-side list, the excess scalars are ignored. For example, if we have

```
($a, $b) = (2, 4, 6);
```

the 6 is ignored. If there are more variables in the target list than scalars in the right-side list, the excess variables are set to undef. For example, in

```
($a, $b, $c) = (2, 4);
```

$a is set to 2, $b is set to 4, and $c is set to undef.

If one of the elements of the target list is an array name, it devours the remainder of the right-side list. For example, in

```
($a, @list, $b) = ("broncos", "chargers", "raiders", "beatles");
```

$a is set to "broncos", @list gets the rest of the right-side list, and $b is set to undef. Because of this greedy behavior, in an assignment statement, array names should only appear in the last position of a target list.

The first element of an array can be conveniently removed and set to a scalar variable by using a scalar and an array together in a list as the target of an assignment, as in

```
($first, @list) = @list;
```

If the value of @list was ("able", "baker", "charlene"), this sets $first to "able" and @list to ("baker", "charlene").

If an array name appears in a list literal that is not the target in an assignment statement, it is expanded to a list of its scalar values. For example, if the value of @list is (2, 4, 6),

```
(1, @list, 10)
```

has the value

```
(1, 2, 4, 6, 10)
```

An array can be set to empty by assigning it the empty list literal (), as in

```
@list = ();
```

An array can also be set to empty with the undef operator, as in

```
undef @list;
```

If you assign undef to an array, as in

```
@list = undef;
```

you do not get an empty array; rather, you get an array of one element, that element being undef. Although there are no multidimensional arrays in Perl, they can be simulated with arrays that store lists of references, as discussed in Chapter 5. Next, we discuss how individual elements of arrays can be referenced and changed.

4.4   REFERENCING ARRAY ELEMENTS

Array elements can be assigned and referenced by attaching subscripts to the array's names. Subscripts for Perl arrays are delimited by brackets ([]). The subscripts themselves are specified with scalar-valued expressions that are coerced, if necessary, to integers. The first subscript in every array is zero, so the highest subscript is one less than the length of the array. Having the subscripts begin at zero is a nod to the implementation, which uses subscript values as offsets to compute the addresses of specific elements. When compared with other programming languages, Perl is a bit odd in that the array name in a reference to an element is specified as if it were a scalar name; that is, it begins with a dollar sign. This of course makes sense, because the elements of an array are themselves scalars. For example, if `@list` is an array of at least six elements, we could have

```
$list[0] = 17;
$sum += $list[5];
```

Even though there appears to be a relationship between the variable names `@list` and `$list`, be careful to avoid thinking there is. Even if there were a scalar variable in the program named `$list` (which would of course be foolish), the use of the name `$list` with a subscript would not affect that scalar variable. For example, consider the following code:

```
$list = "Darcie";
@list = (2, 4, 6, 8);
$list[1] = 10;
print "Scalar: $list  Element: $list[1]  List: @list";
```

The output of this code is

```
Scalar: Darcie  Element: 10  List: 2 10 6 8
```

Array element names can appear in list literals, both as targets and right sides of assignments, as in

```
($list[0], $list[1]) = ($list[1], $list[0]);
```

which interchanges the first two elements of `@list`. This works because list assignments are in effect done in parallel, not one at a time. Note that this interchange also works for any scalar variables in lists, as in

```
($my_salary, $your_salary) = ($your_salary, $my_salary);
```

An access to an element of an array that is beyond the last element returns `undef`. For example, in

```
@highs = (92, 84, 81, 79, 85);
$Saturday_hi = $highs[6];
```

`$Saturday_hi` is set to `undef`. No error message is produced by this statement.

Unlike in most other languages, a reference to an array element with a negative subscript value is valid. Rather than causing an error, the subscript is used as if it were indexing from the high end of the array, counting the last element as a subscript of `-1`. It is as if the subscript range wrapped around from the bottom end to the top end. The element considered to be to the immediate left of the element at subscript zero is the one at subscript `-1`, which is the last element in the array. For example, consider the following;

```
@list = (2, 4, 6, 8, 10);
print "The last element is: $list[-1] \n";          # displays 10
print "The second last element is: $list[-2] \n";   # displays 8
print "The first element is: $list[-5] \n";         # displays 2
```

Assignments to array elements using negative subscript values work the same way. So, a negative subscript value creates a fatal runtime error only if it refers to an element that does not already exist. For example, if `@list` is defined as in the preceding code above (i.e., to have five elements), then

```
$list[-10] = 17;
```

causes a runtime error.

An assignment to an element of an array that is beyond the last currently existing element (using a positive subscript) causes the implicit extension of the array to the required length. For example, if @list currently has five elements,

```
$list[50] = 22;
```

extends the array to a length of 51.

It is sometimes convenient to know the index of the last element of an array. If the array's name is @list, the implicit variable $#list has the index of the last element of a list. For example, the last index of @list can be displayed with

```
print "The last index of \@list is $#list \n";
```

This last index name can also be used to set an array to empty, as in

```
$#list = -1;
```

A program that has an array that grows many times during execution will run faster if the array is extended to its expected maximum length at the beginning of the program. For example, suppose an array in a particular program is expected to eventually grow to a length of 1,000 elements, we can force the array to have that many elements by setting the name of its highest index to 999 (or assigning to its 1,000th element) at the beginning of the program. This will prevent the possibly numerous extensions caused by the program to eventually force the array to that length. For example, for the array @list, either of the following two assignments will extend the array to have 1,000 elements:

```
$list[999] = 0;

$#list = 999;
```

4.5   AN EXAMPLE

The sample program that follows illustrates some of the features of arrays we have discussed so far. In this example, new names must be inserted into a sorted array of names that are read from a file. The method is to compare the new names with the names in the array, starting at the end of the list. Every comparison that finds a name in the array that belongs after the new name causes the name in the array to be moved down one position. When the correct position is found, the new name is inserted into the array. The size of the array of names increases by one every time a new name is inserted.

```
# merge
#  Input: A list of names in ascending order from the file
#         specified on the command line. Also, from the keyboard
#         a second list of names in no particular order
# Output: The ordered list (from the file) with all of the
#         names from the second list (from the keyboard)
#         inserted in their proper positions into the first
#         list (duplicate names in the list are ok)

# Get the first list of names from the file into an array
```

```
$index = 0;

while (chomp($names[$index] = <>)) {
    $index++
}

# Loop to read and insert the names from the second list
# The process is to move names down, starting at the bottom,
# until the position for the new name is found

while (chomp($new_name = <STDIN>)) {

    for ($index = $#names;
         $index >= 0 and $names[$index] gt $new_name;
         $index--){
        $names[$index + 1] = $names[$index]
    }   ##- end of for

# Now insert the new name (it goes at $index+1, because
# $index gets decremented after the last move)

    $names[$index + 1] = $new_name;
} ##- end of while

# Print the resulting list

print "\n The complete list \n\n";

for ($index = 0; $index <= $#names; $index++) {
    print "$names[$index] \n";
}
```

This example shows some of the flexibility of Perl's arrays. The program need not know how long the resulting list of names might be. The array simply grows whenever a new name is added.

Parts of arrays called slices can be treated as units in Perl.

4.6 SLICES

A *slice* of an array is a reference to some subset of the elements of that array. A slice is specified by the array name and a subsequence of the array's range of subscripts, in brackets. For example, consider the following statement:

```
@salaries = (34000, 41950, 52100, 39650);
@salaries[4, 5] = (48500, 41500);
@first3_salaries = @salaries[0, 1, 2];
@next3_salaries = @salaries[3..5];
```

The first assignment statement initializes @salaries to four elements. The second adds two elements at the end. The third assigns the first three elements of @salary to be the value of @first3_salaries. The last assignment statement assigns the last three elements of @salaries to be the value of @next3_salaries.

The subscripts in a slice can be specified individually, or if they are contiguous, using a range operator. The list of subscripts in a slice specification can include expressions. Because a slice is an array, not a scalar, its name begins with @.

Slices of list literals can also be specified. For example, suppose $first and $second are computed by the program and have values in the range of 0 to 4. Then

```
@list = (1, 3, 5, 7, 9)[$first, $second];
```

puts the two list literal elements indexed by the values of $first and $second into @list.

Two elements of an array can be interchanged by using slices, as in

```
@list = (2, 4, 6, 8);
@list[1, 3] = @list[3, 1];   # Now @list is (2, 8, 6, 4)
```

In Chapter 2, we discussed how scalar variables in double-quoted strings were interpolated, which means that their values are substituted for their names. If the name of an array appears in a double-quoted string, it too is interpolated. The values of the elements of the array are converted to string values, if necessary, and catenated together using a single space between the values. One common use of this is in the string parameter to print. For example,

```
@names = ("pooh", "tigger", "piglet", "rabbit");
print "The names are: @names \n";
```

produces the line

```
The names are: pooh tigger piglet rabbit
```

Now that we know what lists and arrays are, we can discuss the concept of scalar and list context in Perl code. Knowing the difference is essential to the effective use of arrays and lists.

4.7   SCALAR AND LIST CONTEXT

It is important to understand that Perl determines values of operands in expressions in part by the context of the operand. The two primary contexts are scalar and list, or array. The simplest situation is an assignment statement, in which the type of the left side, or target, determines the context and thus the form of the right side value. As we saw in Section 4.3, if the target is a scalar and the right side is a list or an array, that list or array will be coerced to a scalar. In this case, the assigned scalar value is the size of the right-side list or array.

Likewise, we saw that if the target of an assignment statement is an array or list, the context of the right-side is list. So, if the right side is a scalar, it is coerced to a list of one element (that scalar value).

Some functions and operators require their parameters or operands to be scalars; some require lists. We will point this out when we describe such functions and operators.

In the case of array names in expressions, the context can be implicitly forced to scalar by making it the operand of a scalar operator, as in

```
@list + 0
```

which evaluates to the length of @list. Scalar context also can be explicitly forced with the pseudofunction, scalar, the purpose of which is exactly this. This is convenient for printing the length of an array, as in

```
print "Length of \@list is: ", scalar(@list), "\n";
```

where print takes a list of strings as its operand, so the commas separating the three elements of the operand in the function do just that: separate the elements; they are not operators in any sense. We used this list form of parameter to print in this example because we had to keep the call to scalar outside the string literal. (Otherwise it would not be called.)

A list literal cannot be forced to scalar context. If a list literal that includes commas is used in scalar context, for example the right side of an assignment to a scalar variable, the value of the list literal is the last element of the list. This is because the last element of a list of expressions separated by commas is the value of the whole expression. For example, in

```
$x = (7, 12, 27, 5);
```

$x is set to 5. However, if a list literal is built with a quote operator, as in

```
$x = qw(a b c d);
```

the value of $x is the number of elements in the list—in this case, 4.

Actually, there is no explicit way to force list context on anything, because any function or operator that requires a list already forces a scalar parameter or operand to be a list.

Some operators work in both scalar and list contexts. For example, we have used the line input operator in scalar context, as in

```
$next = <STDIN>;
```

When it appears in scalar context, this operator returns the next line of input from the keyboard. We can put the line input operator in list context by assigning it to an array, as in

```
@input = <STDIN>;
```

In this case, all lines of keyboard input are read and assigned to the @input array, one line per element. Another example of an operator that can be used in both scalar or list context is chomp, as discussed in Section 4.9.

4.8   THE foreach STATEMENT

In Chapter 3, we mentioned that there was an iterative statement in Perl whose control is based on the number of elements in an array or list. The foreach statement is actually just an alternative form of the for statement. The word foreach is used because it is slightly more connotative. The general form of foreach is

```
foreach [scalar_variable] (list literal or array name) {
    ...
}
```

The brackets around scalar_variable mean that it is optional. If it is omitted, $_ is used. The scalar variable becomes an alias for the elements of the list or array, one at a time, for the iterations of the loop body (by alias, we mean what you would expect: a second name for whatever it is the alias of.) For example,

```
foreach $age (@ages) {
    $age++
}
```

increments each of the elements of @ages. The scalar variable in a foreach is a special variable that is distinct from any program variable that happens to have the same name. It is local to the loop body. As an example, consider the following statement:

```
$count = 17;

foreach $count (1, 3, 5, 7, 9) {
    $sum += $salaries[$count];
}

print "\$count is: $count \n";
```

The print statement here displays 17, but the value of $count in the loop is 9. A range operator is often used to specify the list in a foreach statement, as in

```
$sum = 0;

foreach $index (0..99) {
    $sum += $list[$index];
}
```

A foreach statement can be labeled, have a continue block, and include any of the control operators, next, last, or redo. A foreach loop typically runs about twice as fast as an equivalent loop written with for.

foreach can be used as a statement modifier. The general syntax of this is

Statement foreach expression,

where expression is a list literal or an array. The implicit variable $_ is set to the values in the expression, as in

```
$sum = 0;
$sum += $list[$_] foreach (0..99);
```

We have now completed our discussion of how to use ordinary scalar operators to manipulate individual array elements. The next subsection describes some of the Perl functions (or operators) that operate on arrays and lists, as well as their elements.

4.9   LIST OPERATORS

Perl includes a collection of operators that manipulate lists and arrays. Because the value of an array is a list, we often refer to these as list operators. Recall that operators can often be treated as functions.

4.9.1 **THE** reverse **OPERATOR**

The reverse operator does what its name implies, reverses the order of the elements of its list operand. For example,

```
@names = ("Al", "Bob", "Jake", "Ezekiel");
@rnames = reverse @names;
print "@rnames \n";
```

displays

```
Ezekiel Jake Bob Al
```

The reverse operator is sometimes used to reverse the order of elements accessed by a foreach, as in

```
foreach $employee (reverse @employee_list) {
    print "$employee\n";
}
```

If reverse is used on a scalar, it coerces it to a string, if necessary, reverses the order of its characters, and returns the result. For example, if $name is "adam", after execution of

```
$rname = reverse $name;
```

the value of $rname is "mada". Note that the value of the operand of reverse, in our example $name, is not affected by this reverse.

4.9.2 **THE** sort **OPERATOR**

The sort operator sorts lists of strings. For example,

```
@names = ("eve", "adam", "devil", "worm");
@sorted_names = sort @names;
print "Sorted list of names is: @sorted_names \n";
```

displays

```
Sorted list of names is: adam devil eve worm
```

If you inadvertently use sort on a list of numbers, they are coerced to strings and sorted as strings, which is probably not what you wanted. For example,

```
@list = (42, 68, 10, 5, 103);
@sorted_list = sort @list;
print "Sorted list is: @sorted_list \n";
```

displays

```
Sorted list is: 10 103 42 5 68
```

The sort operator can be used to sort all kinds of lists into whatever order we choose, but we delay discussion of this form of sort until Chapter 6, because it requires some knowledge of writing Perl functions.

4.9.3 THE REPETITION OPERATOR

The repetition operator (x) introduced in Chapter 2 as a string operator also works for lists. For example,

```
@valentine = ("I love you!") x 5;
```

This creates an array of five elements, each of which is the string "I love you!". All of the elements of an array can be set using the repetition operator, as in

```
@list = (0) x @list;
```

This use of @list on the right side is the length of @list because the right operand of x is a scalar.

4.9.4 THE chop AND chomp OPERATORS

The chop and chomp operators can take lists, as well as scalars, as operands. When given a list, chomp removes the line separators from the ends of all of the elements of the list (that end in line separators) and returns the total number of separators it removed. When given a list, chop removes the last character from the ends of all of the elements of the list and returns the last character it removed. For example,

```
@list = ('little', 'green', 'apples');
chop(@list);
```

puts ('littl', 'gree', 'apple') in @list and returns 's'.

4.9.5 THE splice FUNCTION

The splice function provides a powerful tool for modifying arrays. It can be used to re-move a slice from an array and optionally replace the removed elements with a possi-bly different number of new elements. In most other languages, removing an element or adding an element to the interior of an array is a relatively complicated operation. The splice function makes those operations very simple.

splice can take a variable number of parameters, among which only the first two are mandatory: an array and an offset from the base of that array. Given just these two parameters, splice removes all elements from the array—from the one with the spec-ified offset to the end. For example,

```
@list = (2, 4, 6, 8, 10);
splice (@list, 3);
print "\@list is now: @list \n";
```

produces

```
@list is now: 2 4 6
```

The optional third parameter to splice, when given, is the number of elements to be removed from the array. For example,

```
@list = (2, 4, 6, 8, 10);
splice (@list, 2, 2);
print "\@list is now: @list \n";
```

produces

```
@list is now: 2 4 10
```

The optional fourth parameter to `splice` can be an array, in which case its elements replace the removed elements from the array. For example,

```
@list = (1, 2, 3, 4, 5);
@new = (7, 6);
splice (@list, 2, 2, @new);
print "\@list is now: @list \n";
```

produces

```
@list is now: 1 2 7 6 5
```

This also works when the call to `splice` specifies that no elements are to be removed, as in

```
@list = (1, 2, 3, 4, 5);
@new = (7, 6);
splice (@list, 2, 0, @new);
print "\@list is now: @list \n";
```

which produces

```
@list is now: 1 2 7 6 3 4 5
```

Finally, a call to `splice` can specify any number of scalars, in place of the fourth array parameter. In this case, `splice` behaves as if an array whose contents were the scalars had been specified. For example.

```
@list = (1, 2, 3, 4, 5);
splice (@list, 2, 2, 9, 8, 7);
print "\@list is now: @list \n";
```

produces

```
@list is now: 1 2 9 8 7 5
```

4.9.6   THE pop AND push FUNCTIONS

Some of `splice`'s array operations are so commonly used that Perl includes separate functions to provide them. These are for adding and removing single elements from one of the ends of an array. A stack is a common linear data structure in which all additions and removals of data are from one end. Stacks can be, and often are, simulated with arrays, by using the first element of the array as the stack's bottom element and its last useful element for the stack's top element. In Perl, stack operations on an array being used as a stack can be specified for arrays using `splice`. A more convenient method is to use the two functions (operators), `push` and `pop`, which are the traditional names of the stack addition and removal operations. In many other languages, a user implementation of a stack in an array requires maintenance of the variable that stores the currrent location in the array of the stack's top. In Perl, this is not necessary, because Perl keeps track of the length of all arrays.

The `push` operator takes two operands, an array name and a value that is to be placed in the array. For example,

```
push @stack1, "Mary";
```

inserts `"Mary"` into `@stack1` just after its last element. The second operand could be a list or an array name. In these cases, all elements of the second operand are placed on the end of the array. For example, consider the following statement:

```
@stack1 = (1, 3, 5, 7);
push @stack1, (9, 11, 13);
```

Now, the contents of `@stack1` are 1, 3, 5, 7, 9, 11, 13. The list operand of `push` need not be parenthesized, as illustrated in

```
push @stack1, 9, 11, 13;
```

If this form of the second parameter is used, we prefer to treat `push` as a function, as in

```
push(@stack1, 9, 1, 13);
```

The other fundamental stack operation is the removal of the top element. The Perl `pop` operator performs this by removing the last element of its array operand and returning it. For example, using the array we just built, `@stack1`,

```
$value = pop @stack1;
print "The popped value is: $value \n";
```

displays

```
The popped value is: 13
```

The `pop` operator returns `undef` if the operand array is empty. Because `pop` and `push` deal with the high-subscript end (or top) of an array, it is most natural to think of stacks as being vertical, with their high-subscript end at the top.

4.9.7   THE `unshift` AND `shift` FUNCTIONS

The `unshift` and `shift` functions do the same things `pop` and `push` do, but to the bottom, or low-subscript end, of an array, as illustrated in the code:

```
@list = ("bob", "carol", "ted", "alice");
$name = shift @list;
print "The shifted off name is: $name \n";
unshift @list, "mikie";
unshift @list, ("beanie", "baby");
print "The new list is: @list \n";
```

This displays

```
The shifted off name is: bob
The new list is: beanie baby mikie carol ted alice
```

As with `pop`, `shift` returns `undef` if its operand is an empty array.

Arrays can be rotated left conveniently with the `push` and `unshift` operators. For example,

```
push @list, shift(@list);
```

rotates `@list` left. Similarly, `pop` and `unshift` can be used to rotate an array right, as in

```
unshift @list, pop(@list);
```

4.9.8 THE `split` FUNCTION

Perl includes a function, `split`, for taking strings apart. We postponed discussing it in Chapter 2, because the result of `split` is often assigned to an array. A call to `split` can appear in several forms:

```
split /Pattern/, Expression, Limit
split /Pattern/, Expression
split /Pattern/
split
```

The Pattern parameter is a regular expression, which is discussed in detail in Chapter 7. For now, we will deal with only the simplest regular expressions, those that consist of a single character or nothing at all. Regular expressions are often delimited by slashes, which is the form of the Pattern parameter to `split`. For example, `/:/` specifies a pattern that is the single character, `:`. When used as a parameter to `split`, this pattern specifies that the given string, specified by Expression, is to be split at every colon. All of the substrings created by `split` are returned in a list. The Limit parameter specifies the maximum number of substrings that `split` should produce. For example,

```
@fruit = split /,/, "apples,gwapes,pineapples,cannonballs", 3;
```

sets `@fruit` to `("apples", "gwapes", "pineapples,cannonballs")`. Note that the last string in the value of `@fruit` includes all of the remaining string (after the two splits have taken place). When there is no match, `split` returns the Expression string.

If the Limit parameter is absent, the entire string is split into all of its parts. If the Expression is absent, the implicit variable `$_` is used. If the Pattern parameter and the Expression are absent, the split is done on `$_`, using whitespace as the separator. For example,

```
$_ = "J. Edgar Hoover";
($first_name, $middle_name, $last_name) = split;
```

puts `"J."` into `$first_name`, `"Edgar"` into `$middle_name`, and `"Hoover"` into `$last_name`.

Note that you cannot have an Expression parameter for `split` without also having a Pattern parameter (because the Expression will be used as the Pattern). If the Pattern is the empty string, `split` splits the given string into its individual characters. For example,

```
@chars = split //, "kumquats";
```

puts `("k", "u", "m", "q", "u", "a", "t", "s")` into `@chars`.

If `split` is called in scalar context, for example if the call to `split` is the right side of an assignment to a scalar variable, it returns the number of substrings into which the given string was split. If there was no match of the Pattern, `split` returns 1.

As stated, the Pattern operand of `split` can be any Perl regular expression, which could be highly complex. The structure of these regular expressions and the general process of pattern matching are described in Chapter 7.

4.10 AN EXAMPLE

The sample program that follows illustrates the use of some of the functions described in Section 4.9. For each line of text in a given file, it changes the first letter in each word to uppercase and displays the new line. The split function is used to separate the line into its words. Then split is used on each word to separate it into an array of its letters. Then uc is used to change the first letter to uppercase. The join function is used to put the words and the line back together.

```
# caps
#  Input: A file of text, specified on the command line, in which
#          the words in the lines are separated by single spaces
# Output: The lines of text from the file, with the first letter

#          of each word capitalized

# Loop to process all lines in the file

while (chop($line = <>)) {

# Split the line into its words

    @words = split / /, $line;

# Loop to convert the first letters of all words to uppercase

    foreach $word (@words) {

# Convert the word to an array of letters and convert the first letter

        @chars = split //, $word;
        $chars[0] = uc($chars[0]);

# Put the word back together

        $word = join('', @chars);
    } ##- end of foreach

# Put the line back together

    $line = join(' ', @words);
    print "New line: $line \n";
} ##- end of while
```

4.11 COMMAND-LINE ARGUMENTS

Now that we have discussed arrays, we can describe how command-line arguments[2] can be accessed in a program. Programs can be parameterized by passing them parameters on the command line that specifies the execution of perl. During program execution,

---

[2]I know, I know, I said we would call things like these parameters. But the long tradition in the UNIX world of calling them arguments does not permit me to change their name here.

the predefined array, @ARGV, contains the command-line arguments that appeared on the command line which ran the perl system. Similarly to other arrays, the implicit variable $#ARGV contains the subscript of the last element in @ARGV. The command-line arguments could simply be accessed using indexing on that array. For example, to list the command-line arguments, one could use

```
foreach $index (0 .. $#ARGV) {
    print "$ARGV[$index] \n";
}
```

In many cases, the command-line arguments are removed from @ARGV as needed by using shift. All of the command-line arguments can be printed by using shift with

```
$num_args = $#ARGV + 1;

for ($count = 1; $count <= $num_args; $count++) {
    $argument = shift(@ARGV);
    print "$argument \n";
}
```

You might be tempted to avoid defining $num_args in this code, and use $count <= $#ARGV + 1 for the for control expression. However, this will not work, because shift causes $#ARGV to be decremented each time the loop body is executed.

If either pop or shift appears without an operand in a Perl program outside a function definition, the default operand is @ARGV. So, in the preceding code, we could have gotten the command-line arguments with

```
$argument = shift;
```

instead of

```
$argument = shift(@ARGV);
```


4.12   SUMMARY

A list literal is a sequence of values, delimited by parentheses, used to specify a list in a program. A range operator can also be used to specify a list of either numbers, characters, or even multiple characters. Array variable names are distinguished from scalar names by the rule that they begin with at signs (@). Arrays can be assigned other arrays or lists. Lists of scalar variable names can also be assigned arrays or literal lists. If an array is assigned to a scalar, the length of the array is assigned.

Array elements are referenced by using the scalar version of the array's name and attaching a subscript. Array subscripts, which can be any scalar-valued expression that can be coerced to an integer, are delimited with brackets. Array element names can appear as the elements of a list. This form is often used as the left side of an assignment statement. Assigning to an element of an array that currently does not exist causes the array to be expanded to the required length. An array can be emptied by assigning it the empty list. An array can be set to having a particular length by assigning to its name, after attaching a dollar sign and a pound sign to the beginning of that name. A slice of an array is some subsequence of its elements, specified either by a list of subscripts or by a range operator.

When the left side of an assignment is a scalar variable, it provides scalar context to the right side. When the left side is an array or list, it provides list context to the right side. Scalar context can be forced with the `scalar` function. Any function (or list operator) that requires a list as a parameter (or operand) forces list context on that parameter (or operand). The input string operator (`<>`) is an example of a function that can operate in either list or scalar context.

Perl includes many list operators (or functions that take lists as parameters). When used on an array, `undef` sets it to empty. The `reverse` operator reverses the order of its list or array operand. It also works on scalar strings, reversing the order of characters in the string. The `sort` operator sorts its operand list or array, interpreting the elements as strings. The repetition infix operator (`x`), when it appears in the proper context, creates multiples of a given list. When used on a list, `chop` removes the last character from each element of the list. When used on a list, `chomp` removes the line separator from the end of every element in the list that has one. The `splice` function can remove and possibly replace slices of arrays. The `push` operator puts its second operand at the end of its first operand, which is an array. The `pop` operator removes and returns the last element of its array operand. The `unshift` and `shift` operators are like `pop` and `push`, but operate on the left end of their array operands. The `split` operator splits a given string into substrings, based on a specified separator string.

4.13   EXERCISES

Write, test, and debug (if necessary) Perl programs for the following problems:

1. Input: A number, *n*, followed by *n* numbers, all from a file specified on the command line.

   Output: The input numbers in descending order.

   Method: Use any sort algorithm you know, but not the Perl `sort` function.

2. Input: A list of numbers in a file specified on the command line.

   Output: Two lists of numbers, one with the input numbers that are greater than zero and one with those that are less than zero (ignore the zero-valued numbers).

   Method: You must first build two arrays with the required output numbers before you display any of them.

3. Input: Two files of numbers, both in ascending order, specified on the command line.

   Output: A list of the numbers in the two input files, all in ascending order.

   Method: You must first build the entire output array before displaying it, and you cannot use any sorting technique (that is, the numbers must be put in the result array one at a time, in their proper places.)

   Hint: The first number from the second file can be identified by it being the first one that is smaller than the previous number.

4.Input: A file containing a list of stack commands, one per line, of the form operation:value, specified on the command line.

Output: A stack, displayed after each command is read and executed.

Notes: The possible commands are push, pop, shift, and unshift. The values can be either strings or numbers.

5. Input: A file that contains English words, where each word is separated from the next word on a line by one space, specified on the command line.

Output: A table, in which the first column has the unique words from the input file and the second column has the number of times the word appeared in the file. No word can appear twice in the table.

Method: Your program must use two arrays to store the table, one for the words and one for the frequency values.

6. Input: A file in which each line has a single number, specified on the command line.

Output: A list of the numbers from the input file, in the same order, but with all negative values removed. (There cannot be any gaps in this file.)

Method: You must build the entire output array, one element at a time, before displaying it.

7. Input: A file in which each line has a single string (which could be a number), specified on the command line.

Output: The median value of all of the numbers in the input file.

Method: You must use `sort` on the array of numbers you build.

8. Input: A file, specified on the command line, in which each line has a word; there will be no more than 100 words.

Output: The input words, both in alphabetical order and reversed alphabetical order.

9. Input: A file, specified on the command line, in which each line has the form: word, number1, number2, character.

Output: The input words, after being modified as follows: The number2-characters, starting at an offset of number1, in each word must be replaced by the given character.

CHAPTER 5

Hashes and References

5.1   **The Structure of Hashes**

5.2   **Operators for Hashes**

5.3   **An Example**

5.4   **References**

5.5   **Nested Data Structures**

5.6   **Another Example**

5.7   **Summary**

5.8   **Exercises**

Outside the world of Perl, hashes are sometimes called associative arrays. They are also sometimes called hash tables, which has been shortened by Perl users to hashes. A hash is a data structure that stores unordered data in a way that allows specific elements to be stored and retrieved very quickly. They are often used for storing dynamic lists of data (lists that grow and shrink during use) which must allow fast access to any specific element of the list. Although hashes have been around a long time, Perl is the only widely used language that has built-in hashes.[1]

This chapter also discusses references, which are scalars that are used to store addresses of data values and structures. References are related to the pointers of other programming languages. Perl does not have pointers. References provide a technique for building complex data structures from arrays and hashes, such as arrays of arrays and arrays of hashes.

5.1   THE STRUCTURE OF HASHES

The elements of an array are found through their association with a number called a subscript or index. The subscript value of an element completely specifies the location of that element. Because the elements are always kept in order by their indices, there is no need to store the indices. In Perl, the subscript of the third element of an array is always 2. So, arrays are ordered lists of scalar values that are addressed by numbers that specify locations within the array.

---

[1]Some other languages, for example Java provide hashes through a library. Long before Java appeared, hashes were implemented with the use of arrays and user-written hash functions in a wide variety of other languages.

Hashes, like arrays, are lists of scalar values. The two fundamental differences between hashes and arrays are as follows:

1.   Rather than numeric indices, the data elements of hashes are indexed by string values called keys, which are also stored in the structure.

2.   The data elements of hashes are not ordered in the structure in which they are stored.

Each element of a hash is a pair of scalar values, the first is the key and the second is the value, or data of the element. Because the elements of a hash are found through the keys, the actual order of data elements is irrelevant. In fact, there is no way your program can determine the order in which the elements are stored in a hash. The Perl system uses an internal hash function to store and retrieve the elements of a hash. A hash function operates on a key string to compute a specific address within the hash structure. Although the more formal name for these structures is associative arrays, because of the use of the hash function—and because it is much easier to say and write—we will always call them hashes.

There is no such thing as a hash literal. List literals are used when you really want a hash literal, as in

```
("bob", 42, "carol", 40, "ted", 29, "jezabel", 71)
```

The symbol => can be used in place of the comma in a list literal, used to specify a hash to make it more readable, as illustrated here:

```
("bob" => 42, "carol" => 40, …)
```

If the left operand of => is a bareword string, it is implicitly quoted. Even if the left operand is a list operator, such as `print`, as in

```
(print => "yes")
```

it will be evaluated as a simple string.

The names of hash variables begin with percent signs (%), so they, like scalars and arrays, have their own namespace. Like arrays, hashes need not be declared, grow as necessary, and can be made to shrink at any time.

Hash variables can be assigned arbitrary even-length lists, specified with list literals or the names of other hashes or arrays. As an example, consider this code:

```
@list = ("Grumpy" => 44, "Sleepy" => 27, "Maxine" => 79);

%dwarfs_ages = @list;

%salaries = ("Bill"  =>  79_500,  "Billy"  =>  43_000,  "Billie"  =>
            55_200, "Billiam" => 14_444);
```

When an array is assigned to a hash, the odd-subscripted elements (the second, fourth, sixth,…elements) of the array become the keys of the hash. A hash can be assigned to an array, but remember that the element pairs of the hash will appear in the array in an unpredictable order. For example, if the hash %salaries were assigned to @pay, the value of pay might be

```
("Billy", 43000, "Billiam", 14444, "Bill", 79500, "Billie", 55200)
```

The individual value elements of a hash can be accessed by "subscripting," using the value's key in braces (not brackets, as with arrays). For example,

```
$salaries{"Billy"}
```

is

```
43000
```

Likewise, new values can be inserted and old values changed by using this mechanism, as in

```
$salaries{"Willie"} = 51_950;
```

If the subscript of a reference to an element of a hash is a bareword string, it is implicitly quoted. For example,

```
$salaries{Billie} += 500;
```

is equivalent to

```
$salaries{"Billie"} += 500;
```

As with arrays, a hash can be set to empty either by setting it to the empty list or by using the undef operator, as in

```
%salaries = ();

undef %salaries;
```

Assigning undef to a hash does *not* set it to empty. Rather, it sets it to have one element, undef. Besides probably not being what you wanted, building a hash with any odd number of elements generates a warning from perl.

Hash variables are not interpolated in quoted strings. If they were, it would conflict with the use of % in the format code parameter to printf. So,

```
print "%salaries \n";
```

displays

```
%salaries
```

rather than the values in that hash.

If you happen to use a bare (nonquoted) hash variable as the parameter to print, as in

```
print %salaries;
```

all of the scalars in the hash, keys and values, are displayed together (with no separating spaces).

A slice of a hash is specified with a list of keys in braces. Such a slice is an array of the values associated with the specified keys. For example,

```
@some_salaries = @salaries {"Bill", "Billiam"};
```

sets @some_salaries to (79500, 14444).

Notice that the slice itself uses the array form of the name of the hash. Because a slice of a hash is an array, it is interpolated if it appears in a double-quoted string.

5.2 OPERATORS FOR HASHES

Perl includes a collection of operators that make using hashes simple and convenient. Elements are removed from a hash with the `delete` operator. The operand to `delete` is the scalar name of the hash with the key of the element that is to be deleted in braces. Both the key and its associated value are removed from the hash. For example,

```
delete $salaries{"Billie"};
```

deletes both `"Billie"` and his salary from `%salaries`.

Using `undef` on a hash key is usually a mistake. It leaves the key in the hash—only the value associated with the key will be undefined.

The `exists` operator is used to determine whether a particular hash element is present in a hash. For example, consider the following code:

```
if (exists $salaries{"Billie"}) {
    print "Billie's_salary is: $salaries{'Billie'} \n";
else {
    print "Billie is not in the salary list \n"
}
```

It is frequently convenient to consider either the keys or values of a hash as an array. The `keys` operator returns a list of the key values from its hash operand. For example,

```
%highs = ("mon" => 64, "tue" => 66, "wed" => 72, "thu" => 55,
          "fri" => 35);
@days = keys %highs;
```

puts (`"mon"`, `"tue"`, `"wed"`, `"thu"`, `"fri"`) into `@days`.

To display the values in the hash `%highs`, we could use the following code:

```
foreach $day (keys %highs) {
    print "On $day the high temperature was $highs{$day} \n";
}
```

This displays the temperatures on all of the days in the hash, but they come out in the order in which they were stored (through the hash function), which is somewhat random. We could add a `sort` operator, as in

```
foreach $day (sort (keys %highs)) {  … }
```

But the preceding code does not do what we probably wanted, because now the days come out in alphabetical order, which is not the order that the days are usually seen. Getting them into their "normal" order is messier than is justified by our level of interest right now, so we will leave them in alphabetical order.

The `keys` operator returns the empty list if its operand is an empty hash. If `keys` is used in scalar context, it returns the number of elements in the hash operand, counting a key and its value as one element. For example,

```
$length = keys %highs;
```

assigns 5 to `$length`.

The values of a hash are extracted and put in a list with the `values` operator, as in

```
foreach $temp (values %highs) {  print "$temp \n" }
```

This produces the list of temperatures, but in a nonsensical order and without the days, which may not be very useful.

Sometimes we prefer to process the pairs of a hash, rather than just the keys or just the values. For such use, Perl has the each operator, which returns a two-element list of the next element of the hash operand. This operator can be used to iterate through an entire hash in what appears to be random order. If each is called on a hash after it has returned all of the elements, it returns the empty list. Thus, the call to each can conveniently be used in the control expression of a while statement to process all of the elements of a hash. Consider the following illustrations:

```
while (($day, $temp) = each %highs) {
    print "On $day the high temperature was $temp \n";
}
```

Elements of the hash can be deleted in a loop such as this. However, elements cannot be added in the loop body. The iterator for a hash is used by each, keys, and values. If either keys or each is called on the hash in the loop body, the iterator is set back to the beginning for all three, including each. This obviously must be remembered if keys or each is to be used in an each-iterated loop.

If a hash is used as a Boolean expression, which is always in scalar context, the result is true if the hash is not empty. The returned value on a nonempty hash is a parameter of the internal hashing operation on the specified hash variable. Because of the rarity of its usefulness, we do not discuss it further here.

Perl has a predefined hash, %ENV, which stores operating system environment variables. These environment variables store a variety of information about the system on which the Perl program is running. The values in %ENV can be accessed as with any hash. We will make use of %ENV in our discussion of CGI programming in Chapter 9. Hashes are also used in connection with DBM databases in UNIX, as we will discuss in Chapter 10.

If many accesses to specific elements are required, a hash is much better than an array, because the implicit hashing operation used to access hash elements is very efficient. Furthermore, hashes are much more convenient than arrays for many uses. This is illustrated with the next example.

5.3 AN EXAMPLE

Suppose that your program reads a file of text in which there may be many duplicate words. Further suppose that the objective of the program is to produce a word frequency table for the words found in the file. A hash is the perfect structure to store the unique words. The unique words can be the keys, and their frequencies can be the values. For each input word, the program can use the exists function on the hash to determine whether the word is already there. If it is, its frequency is incremented. If it is not, it is inserted, and its frequency is set to 1.

If the words were stored in an array, every new word would require a search of the array, which would be more complicated to code and also much slower. This is illustrated here:

```
# word_freq

#     Input:   A file of text in which all words are separated by white
#              space, specified on the command line
#     Output:  A list of all unique words in the input file, in alphabetical
#              order, along with their frequencies of occurrences in the
#              file

# Main loop to get and process lines of input text

while (<>) {

# Split the line into words

    @line_words = split;

# Loop to count the words (either increment or initialize to 1)

    foreach $word (@line_words) {
        if (exists $freq{$word}) {
            $freq{$word}++;
        } else {
            $freq{$word} = 1;
        }

    } ##- end of foreach

} ##- end of while

# Display the words and their frequencies

print "\n Word \t\t Frequency \n\n";

foreach $word (sort keys %freq) {
    print " $word \t\t $freq{$word} \n";

}
```

Note the implicit use of $_ for the input lines and as the operand of split. Also, recall that split with no operands splits $_ by using white space.

5.4 REFERENCES

Next we discuss the third kind of scalar value—references—which are related to the pointers in other programming languages. Many applications require data structures more complex than arrays and hashes. These can be defined and manipulated by using the constant pointers, usually called references, provided in Perl. References are scalar variables whose values are addresses. These addresses can be of other named or anonymous variables (literals), or even subprograms, as we discuss in Chapter 6. Anonymous variables do not have names and can only be used through references.

5.4.1 HARD REFERENCES

A variable used to store a reference is set to the address of a named variable with the backslash operator. For example, consider the following code:

```
$sum = 0;
$ref_sum = \$sum;
@list = (1, 3, 5, 7);
$ref_list = \@list;
```

The variables `$ref_sum` and `$ref_list` now have the addresses of the variables `$sum` and `@list`, respectively. These kinds of references are called *hard references*. References can also point to literals and functions.

A literal becomes the value of an anonymous variable when its address is assigned to a scalar variable. The address of a literal list is obtained by enclosing the elements in brackets, as in

```
$ref_list = [1, 3, 5, 7];
```

`$ref_list` now has the address of the storage created by the compiler to store the list literal on the right side. The list value is an anonymous variable.

The address of a literal hash value is gotten by enclosing the value in braces, as in

```
$ref_hash = {
  'Bob' => '42',
  'Jake' => '12',
  'Darcie' => '11',
};
```

The address of a scalar literal is obtained by putting a backslash in front of the literal, as in

```
$ref_pi = \3.14159;
```

Dereferencing is a fundamental and frequently used operator on reference variables.

5.4.2 DEREFERENCING

References have two associated values, the usual value (which is an address) and the value at that address. The process of specifying the value at the address of the variable is called *dereferencing*. An undereferenced use of a reference variable is a use of its address value. Dereferencing can be either implicit (meaning that the language processor must determine when dereferencing is required) or explicit (meaning that the programmer must specify dereferencing with some additional operator). In Perl, all dereferencing is explicit, although there are several ways this dereferencing can be specified.

One way to specify dereferencing is by putting the name of the reference variable where the alphanumeric part of a variable name would appear in a use. So, if the reference's name is `$ref_sum`, then `$$ref_sum` specifies the value to which `$ref_sum` refers. For example,

```
$sum = 17;
$ref_sum = \$sum;
print "The sum is: $$ref_sum \n";
```

displays

```
The sum is: 17
```

On the other hand,

```
print "The sum is: $ref_sum \n";
```

displays

```
The sum is: SCALAR(0xb75d3c)
```

which says that the displayed value is a scalar whose hex address is b75d3c, in this particular execution.

Another way to specify dereferencing arrays and hashes is with the arrow infix operator (`->`). The arrow operator is placed between the array or hash reference name and the subscript or key specification. For example, the following two assignment statements are equivalent:

```
$$ref_list[3] = 17;
$ref_list -> [3] = 17;
```

Likewise, the following two hash assignment statements are equivalent:

```
$$ref_hash{'Bob'} = '42';
$ref_hash -> {'Bob'} = '42';
```

In addition to hard references, Perl also allows soft references to named variables.

5.4.3 SOFT REFERENCES

A scalar variable that stores a string which is the name of a defined variable can be used as a reference to that variable. For example, in

```
$sum_name = "sum";
$$sum_name = 17;
```

the variable `$sum` is set to 17. This sort of reference, which is called a *symbolic reference*, or *soft reference*, is a bit dangerous, because one can easily be created accidentally (e.g., simply by incorrectly typing the name of the reference variable, resulting in an existing scalar variable name). To avoid this, the compiler can be told to disallow symbolic references, which is done with a message to the compiler called a *pragma*. Pragmas are not statements—they just convey special instructions to the compiler. The pragma

```
use strict 'refs';
```

tells the compiler to flag as errors all symbolic references in the enclosing block.

As we stated at the beginning of this chapter, references are essential to constructing data structures more complex than arrays and hashes.

5.5 NESTED DATA STRUCTURES

A two-dimensional array can be implemented in Perl as an array of references to arrays. For example, an array of references to anonymous arrays of numbers can be constructed with

```
@mat = (
    [1, 3, 5],
    [7, 9, 11],
    [13, 15, 17],
);
```

Note that @mat is an array of references to arrays; it is not itself a reference. The brackets surrounding the three lists of numbers create the references.

An alternative to this is a reference to an array of references to arrays. Both the array of references to rows and the rows themselves can be anonymous. In both cases, brackets create the references, as in

```
$ref_mat = [
    [1, 3, 5],
    [7, 9, 11],
    [13, 15, 17],
];
```

Remember that a list is created with parentheses, as with the @mat array. References are created with brackets, as with $ref_mat. So, $ref_mat is a reference to an anonymous array of references to anonymous arrays. It is not an array.

Suppose the arrays that we want to be the rows of a two-dimensional array already exist, for example,

```
@row1 = (1, 3, 5);
@row2 = (7, 9, 11);
@row3 = (13, 15, 17);
```

In this case, an array of references to those rows could be defined with

```
@mat = (\@row1, \@row2, \@row3);
```

The elements of an array of arrays, such as @mat (not a reference to an array, such as $mat_ref), can be referenced by using subscripts and the arrow operator, as is illustrated here:

```
print "The (2,3) element is: $mat[2] -> [3] \n";
```

The arrow operator is optional between bracketed or braced expressions. So, the following statement is equivalent to the preceding version:

```
print "The (2,3) element is: $mat[2][3] \n";
```

In the case of a reference to an array of references to arrays, such as the aforementioned $ref_mat, the assignment statements

```
$ref_mat -> [2][2] = 17;
$$ref_mat[2][2] = 17;
```

are equivalent, although the first is easier to understand. The second uses the fact that the $ dereferencing operator has a higher precedence than the brackets around the subscripts. This means $$ref_mat is interpreted as a reference to a two-dimensional array, rather than `$ref_mat[2]` being interpreted as a reference to a single-dimensioned array. Remember that in both of these assignment statements, there is an implied arrow operator between the pairs of subscripts.

In Perl, unlike some other programming languages, an array of references to arrays is not interchangeable with a reference to an array of references to arrays (in other words, a reference to a two-dimensional array).

One characteristic of Perl's two-dimensional arrays that distinguishes them from their counterparts in other programming languages is that they grow when necessary. Related to this is the fact that Perl arrays are never declared. Consider the following code:

```perl
$num_rows = <STDIN>;

foreach $row_num (0 .. $num_rows - 1) {
    $temp = <STDIN>;
    @row = split / /, $temp;
    $mat[$row_num] = [ @row ];
}
```

This code gets lines from the keyboard, splits them on blank delimiters into literals (numbers or strings), and puts the literals from each input line into a row of the two-dimensional array `@mat`. Each row can have any length. The brackets around `@row` in the last line of the aforementioned code create a reference to a new anonymous array that has the elements of `@row`. If the brackets were not included, the length of `@row` would be assigned to `$mat[$row]`, because of the scalar context of the right side of the assignment.

It would also be incorrect to use `\@row` as the right side of that last assignment statement. That would assign the address of `@row`, which is a constant, to each element of `@mat`.

The preceding two-dimensional array can be printed with

```perl
foreach $ref_row ( @mat ) {
    print "@$ref_row";
}
```

One can use references to implement hashes of arrays, hashes of hashes, arrays of hashes, or more complicated structures. The example that follows illustrates the use of an array of hashes.

A user group could keep its members in an array of hashes, in which each array element represents a member. This array could be initialized with

```perl
@members = (
    { name => "Red North",
      email => 'rnorth@fuzzball.ucc.edu',
      phone => "5551221",
    },
    { name => "Fred South",
      phone => "5551234",
    },
    { name => "Ted East",
      email => 'teast@megan.com',
```

```
    },
    { name => "Ed West",
      phone => "5554321",
      pager => "5551111",
    },
    };
```

Notice that the individual hash elements do not have the same collection of keys—that is why an array of arrays is not convenient for this situation. The following code prints the contents of the @members array:

```
for $index (0 .. $#members) {
    print "Member $index is: ";

    for $memberfield(keys % {$members[$index]}) {
        print "$memberfield = $members[$index]{$memberfield}";
}
    print "\n";
}
```

As an example of a hash of hashes, consider the following situation: The names of teams and their star members must be stored. For example, for football, we might have

```
%teams = (
  Broncos => {
          quarterback => "Elway",
          runningback => "Davis",
          tight_end => "Sharp",
          },

  Packers => {
          quarterback => "Favre",
          defensive_end => "White",
          tight_end => "Chmura",
          },

  Forty_Niners => {
          quarterback => "Young",
          wide_receiver => "Rice",
          line_backer => "Norton",
          },
  );
```

The following code prints the data in this structure:

```
while (($team, $position) = each %teams) {
    print "$team: ";
    while (($position, $player) = each %$position) {
        print "$position: $player";
    }

print "\n";
```

```
}
```

5.6 ANOTHER EXAMPLE

A matrix is a two-dimensional array in which all rows have the same number of elements. The following simple program, in which two matrices of numbers are read from a file and added together and the sum matrix is then displayed, illustrates the use of matrices, implemented by using arrays of arrays:

```perl
# matadd
#  Input: Two numbers, $num_rows and $num_cols, followed by two matrices
#         with those dimensions, of numbers, one row per line, from the
#         file specified on the command line.
# Output: The matrix that is the sum of the two input matrices

# Get the dimensions of the two input matrices

$num_rows = <>;
$num_cols = <>;

# Get the two matrices

foreach $row (0 .. $num_rows - 1) {
    @arow = split / /, <>;
    $mat1[$row] = [ @arow ];
}

foreach $row (0 .. $num_rows - 1) {
    @arow = split / /, <>;
    $mat2[$row] = [ @arow ];
}

# Compute the sum matrix

foreach $row (0 .. $num_rows - 1) {

    foreach $col (0 .. $num_cols - 1) {
        $sum_mat[$row][$col] = $mat1[$row][$col] + $mat2[$row][$col];
    }

}

# Print the sum matrix

print "\n The sum matrix is: \n\n";

foreach $ref_row (@sum_mat) {
    print "@$ref_row \n";
}
```

This program illustrates the simplest kind of use of a nested data structure. In fact, the code looks very much like that of other common programming languages.

5.7 SUMMARY

A hash, or associative array, is a linear data structure in which the elements are logically collected into pairs, with the first component of each pair being the key and the second being a scalar value. Hashes differ from arrays in that element access is through the keys (which are always strings), rather than numeric subscripts, and the pair elements are not ordered as arrays are. The names of hash variables all begin with a percent sign to distinguish them from scalar and array variables. List literals serve as hash literals. To make them more readable, the keys can be separated from the values by the symbol =>, rather than commas. An individual value in a hash is specified by the hash name, followed by the associated key in braces. Arrays and list literals can be assigned to hashes, and hashes can be assigned to arrays. As is the case with array elements, an individual element of a hash is specified with a scalar name.

A pair element of a hash can be deleted with `delete`, and `undef` sets a hash to empty. The `exists` operator is used to determine if a particular key is in the hash. The `keys` operator returns an array of the keys from a hash. The `each` operator is used to cycle through all of the elements of a hash in a `foreach` loop.

References are scalar variables whose values are constant pointers. They are set by using the backslash operator on an existing variable or a literal as the right side of an assignment. One way reference variables can be dereferenced is by preceding their names with a dollar sign. If the reference is to an array or hash, the arrow operator can be used for dereferencing.

Nested data structures can be built by using arrays or hashes of references. Hashes of arrays, hashes of hashes, arrays of arrays, arrays of hashes, and many other more complex structures can be built by using references.

5.8 EXERCISES

Write, test, and debug (if necessary) Perl programs for the following problems:

1. **Input:** A file in which each line contains a string of the form name+sales, where in some cases the sales will be absent (but not the plus sign), specified on the command line.

   Output: A list of the names and sales numbers that remain after the following processing:

   a. names with sales numbers are added to a hash when they are first found, along with their sales numbers.

   b. names with absent sales numbers are deleted from the hash if they are already there.

   c. when a name appears that is already in the hash, the new sales number is added to the old sales number (the one already in the hash).

2. **Input:** A file containing a number n on the first line, followed by n more lines, each with n-numbers, specified on the command line. The first number is the number of rows and columns of a square matrix. Each line in the rest of the file is a row of the matrix.

3. Repeat Problem 2, but this time you must do all references to all of the arrays through reference variables.

Output: The sums of each of the columns of the input matrix.

Method: You must make all references to the matrix through a reference variable.

4. Input: A file containing lines of text, where each line has two fields, separated by an ampersand (&), specified on the command line. The two fields on each input line are a name and grade-point average.

Output: Two tables, both in alphabetical order by name. The first table has the names of those people whose grade-point averages were above 3.5, along with their grade-point averages. The second table has the other people's names and their grade-point averages.

Method: The two tables must be built in hashes before any output is produced.

5. Input: A file, specified on the command line, in which each line has the name of a student and the grades that the student has received in the current term. The number of grades varies among the students, because of extra-credit homework. All grades are on a scale of 0–100.

Output: A list of all of the students, in alphabetical order, along with their average grades.

Method: You must store the initial data in a hash of arrays before any computation is done.

CHAPTER 6

Functions

The subprograms, or in the case of Perl, the functions of a programming language are among its most important capabilities. Indeed, without subprograms, it is practically impossible to write programs with any significant size or complexity. Therefore, it is essential that a Perl programmer know well the details of Perl functions.

This chapter begins with some general background on subprograms. It then introduces the simplest Perl functions: those without parameters and the most common ways they are called. Next, we introduce the ideas of scopes and lifetimes of variables and how local variables can be defined in functions. After that, we discuss parameter passing in Perl, followed by an explanation of indirect function calls, and a brief introduction to some of Perl's predefined functions, of which there are many.

6.1   FUNDAMENTALS OF SUBPROGRAMS

A subprogram is close to what its name indicates: a unit of code that is not a complete program. Subprograms are used to design and implement programs as collections and often hierarchies of processing units, each of which defines one part of the overall processing of the program. They make large and complex programs feasible by allowing developers to focus on relatively small parts of the complete program, one at a time, rather than needing to consider the whole program as a unit.

Although subprograms that always do exactly the same thing when called are sometimes useful, subprograms are made far more valuable when they can be parameterized. In this latter case, the subprogram can always perform the same process, but potentially on different data each time it is executed.

In Perl, all subprograms are in the form of functions. A function is directed to ex-ecute its code by a call in a program or another function. The call may also provide ac-tual parameter values to the function, which it uses in its computations. Most functions return values based on their computations.

A *function definition* specifies the name of the function, along with a complete de-scription of its actions, in the form of a block. In Perl, the number of parameters, the types of the parameters, and the type of the returned value of a function are not ex-plicitly stated.[1] A *function declaration* states that the specified name is that of a func-tion, but does not include the code that defines its actions. Function declarations are used to inform the compiler that a name is that of a function and that its definition will be provided elsewhere.

Perl functions can be defined anywhere in a program, except inside another func-tion's definition. Some programmers put all function definitions at the end of their pro-grams; others, including us, put them at the beginning. It does not matter to the Perl compiler, because it has no problem with a call to a function that precedes the appear-ance of its definition in the program.

6.2 FUNCTIONS WITHOUT PARAMETERS

We can now begin our discussion of Perl functions, starting with their simplest form. This section describes the forms of the definitions, declarations, and direct calls to func-tions without parameters. Much of the material presented also applies to functions that do have parameters.

6.2.1 DEFINITIONS AND DECLARATIONS

The syntax of the definition of a Perl function is

```
sub function_name Block
```

where Block is a block containing the Perl statements that are executed when the func-tion is called. For example, consider the following code:

```
sub print_header {
    print "\n Program Output \n\n";
}
```

When called, `print_header` skips a line, displays `"Program Output"`, and skips an-other line.

A declaration of `print_header` follows:

```
sub print_header;
```

6.2.2 DIRECT FUNCTION CALLS

This subsection explains direct function calls and the purpose of function declarations. Indirect function calls are discussed in Section 6.6. A function call is an expression, the

---

[1] Actually, Perl allows function prototypes, which do specify parameters and their types, but they are used mainly to write modules and are not discussed in this chapter.

value of which is that returned by the called function. In some situations, the value returned by a function is of no interest to the caller, in which case the function call can stand alone as a statement. Such a call consists of the name of the function, followed by empty parentheses, as in

```
print_header();
```

A function whose definition or declaration previously has been seen by the compiler can be treated as a list operator. For example, after the compiler has seen either a definition or declaration of print_header, it can be called with

```
print_header;
```

So, if a call to a function precedes that function's definition, placing a declaration of the function at the beginning of the program (or anywhere before the call) will allow it to be called with this simpler form. In our examples throughout the book, we will call user-written functions as functions (with the parentheses), rather than treat them as list operators. This saves us from needing to worry about whether the called function has been previously defined or declared. Of course, a call to a function that returns a value of interest to the caller cannot be called as a standalone expression (because the return value would not have a destination). Such a call must either be an operand of an expression or serve as the right side of an assignment statement. For example, in the following statement both fun and sumer return values:

```
$result = 2 * fun() + 1;
$sum = sumer();
```

Technically, a function name is preceded by an ampersand (&), but in most cases the ampersand is optional and is not included. Section 6.6 discusses a situation in which the ampersand *is* required.

6.2.3 VALUES RETURNED FROM FUNCTIONS

The value returned by a function can be specified in the function in two ways. The clearest and most flexible way is to include a call to the predefined function return. The return function takes an expression as a parameter and returns the value of that expression to the caller of the function in which the call to return appears. In the second way, if the execution of a function does not end with a call to return—that is, if execution reaches the end of the function—the returned value is that of the last expression evaluated (not necessarily the last expression that appears in the function). The following two functions, two_pi_1 and two_pi_2, are equivalent:

```
$pi = 3.14159;
sub two_pi_1 {
    return(2 * $pi);
}

sub two_pi_2 {
    2 * $pi;
}
```

The return function can be called from any place in a function. Furthermore, it can be called from more than one place in a function, but that can make the function more difficult to read and understand.

6.2.4 THE CONTEXT OF A FUNCTION CALL

The context of a function call (scalar or list) dictates the context of the evaluation of the returned value, whether or not it is returned by a call to return. For example, consider the following program:

```
sub sub1 {
    @result = (1, 3, 5);
}

$scalar = sub1();   ##- Scalar context
print "Scalar return value from sub1 is: $scalar \n";
@list = sub1();     ##- List context
print "List return value from sub1 is: @list \n";
```

The result of running this program is

```
Scalar return value from sub1 is: 3
List return value from sub1 is: 1 3 5
```

A function can determine the context of its call with the Boolean function wantarray, which returns true if the call's context is list and false if it is scalar. If return includes no parameter, in scalar context it returns undef; in list context, it returns the empty list. All Perl functions can be called recursively; that is, they can call themselves.

6.3   THE SCOPE AND LIFETIME OF A VARIABLE

Before we can discuss functions with parameters, we must describe the characteristics of local variables. This in turn requires an introduction to the concept of the scope and lifetime of a variable. The *scope* of a variable is the range of statements over which the variable is visible—where it can be used. The *lifetime* of a variable begins when it is created and ends when it can no longer be used. Scope is a spatial concept; lifetime is a temporal concept.

All of the variables we have used so far in our examples have been implicitly defined, making them global variables, the scope of which is the whole program file. The lifetime of a global variable is that of the entire program execution. So far we have not even explained how variables can be defined.

Global variables are not appropriate for variables that are only needed inside a function. The problem with using globals for such variables is the possibility of name conflicts with variables outside the function. There is simply no way to write a function and use variable names that are both meaningful and are guaranteed not be the same as some global variable implicitly defined outside the function. This is especially so when the function is reused (in some program other than the one for which it was written) or when different parts of the program are written by different programmers.

6.3.1 LOCAL VARIABLES

Perl provides two functions that create nonglobal variables, my and local. We first discuss variables defined in functions using my.[2] For example, the variable $sum in

```
sub sub1 {
    my $sum = 0;

    ...
}
```

has the scope of the function's block. Its lifetime is from the execution of the my declaration to the end of the execution of that block. For readability's (and sensibility's) sake, all my declarations for function variables should appear at the beginning of the function. That makes them easy to find and also insures that their scope is that of the whole function.

A call to my takes a single parameter, but that parameter can be a list literal, as in

```
my($a, $b, $c);
```

A call to my that uses a list as the actual parameter imposes list context to any assigned initial values. For example, we might have

```
my($a, @list) = (3, 2, 7, 6);
```

which initializes $a to 3 and @list to (2, 7, 6). This need for list context is the only reason to parenthesize local variables in their my declarations. In all other cases, we will use a my declaration for each variable being declared.

Any block can include my declarations. As is the case when the block is the body of a function, the scope of variables defined with my in a block that is not the body of a function is from their definition to the end of the smallest enclosing block. Their lifetime is from the time their my declaration is executed until execution leaves the block in which they are defined. Although function definitions cannot be nested in Perl, any block that is not the body of a function definition can be nested. For example, we could have

```
$temp = 5;
{
    my $temp = 10;
    if ($list[$outer] > $list[$inner]) {
        my $temp = $list[$inner]
        $list[$outer] = $list[$inner];
        $list[$inner] = $temp;
    }
}
```

This code implicitly defines a global variable $temp (with the assignment statement at the top) and two local versions of variables with the same name (with the two my declarations). In the if block, only the version of $temp defined there is visible, although there are different variables named $temp that are live at that time.[3] In the larg-

---

[2] Technically, my is a predefined function (or operator). However, it is practical to talk of it as if it were an executable declaration.

er block, only the version defined there is visible, although the global version is also live then. No use of a variable defined in a block affects the value or values of variables with the same name defined either globally or in enclosing scopes (blocks). A variable whose scope is limited to the block in which it is explicitly defined, which is the case with all my variables, is said to be *static* or *lexical scoped*.

A Perl program can include a pragma that instructs the compiler to disallow any non-static-scoped variables. This pragma is

```
use strict 'vars';
```

Global variables are defined in programs that include this pragma, using my declarations that appear outside any function definition or block. The scope of these variables is from the my declaration to the end of the file. Most special variables, such as $_, are exempt from the requirement imposed by the use of the preceding pragma.

Forcing all program variables to be declared has the advantage of allowing the compiler to detect typing errors in variable names. For example, suppose we type $sun when $sum was intended and the program has no variable named $sun. This results in an error if use strict 'vars' is included, but does not otherwise (because $sun will be implicitly defined as a new global variable by the compiler). Another advantage of my variables is that access to them is slightly faster than access to globals.

Because my is executable, it should nearly never be placed in a loop. If my does appear in a loop, new versions of the variables it defines are created with each iteration, which is rarely useful.

The second way to define nonglobal variables is with local declarations. Variables defined with local have the same lifetime as those defined with my, but their scope is different. We call the variables defined with local semilocal, because of their larger scope. They are visible in the block in which they are defined, and also in any functions called from that block, and any functions called from those functions, and so forth. This is called *dynamic scoping*. Because dynamic scoping makes programs more difficult to understand, we do not recommend its use.

Function names cannot be defined to be local or semilocal; therefore all functions are global. If a program includes two functions with the same name, the latter definition effectively hides the first throughout the program. If the -w option is used to run the program, a warning is produced when this happens.

6.4 PARAMETERS

We can now begin to discuss the parameter-passing mechanism in Perl. *Actual parameters* are those specified in a call to a function; *formal parameters* are the variables in the function that correspond to the actual parameters in the call. Actual parameters are specified within parentheses, following the function's name in a function call.

One technique of passing parameters is called *pass by value*, which means the values of actual parameters are made available to the called function. This method provides one-way communication to the called function. Parameters may also be *pass by reference*, meaning that the address of the actual parameter is made available to the

---

[3] A variable is *live* during its lifetime.

called function. This provides two-way communication to the called function, because the called function can change the values of the actual parameters in the caller. Most languages, Perl included, support both pass-by-value and pass-by-reference parameter passing.

6.4.1 PASS-BY-REFERENCE PARAMETERS

In Perl, parameter transmission to (and possibly from) the called function is through an implicit array variable, @_, or @ARG if you include use English in the program. At the time of a call to a function, the values of the actual parameters specified in the call are copied into @ARG. Just before control is returned to the caller, every actual parameter that was a variable has its potentially new value copied from @ARG back into the variable's storage. Therefore, the implicit parameter passing of Perl is pass by reference.

When an array name is used as an actual parameter, all of its values are copied into @ARG. For example, consider the following call to fun:

```
@list = (1, 3, 5);
fun(6, @list);
```

Inside fun, @ARG has the value

```
(6 1 3 5)
```

An actual parameter that is a hash has its values flattened into an array and copied into @ARG. In @ARG, of course, the hash is just a plain array. Later in this section, we describe how to use a passed hash as a hash (rather than an array) in the called function. The best way to pass a hash as a parameter is by passing a reference to it, as illustrated in Section 6.4.3.

Every function execution has its own version of @ARG. Whenever a function is called from another function, the current version of @ARG is saved and a new one is created for the newly executing function.

It is not a problem to have more actual parameters passed to a function than it uses. For example, if three parameters are passed, but the function never references $ARG[2], that is not any kind of error. If only two parameters are passed and the function references $ARG[2], its value is undef, which is probably a mistake, but no error is noted by the compiler or interpreter.

The elements of @ARG can be used directly. Whatever changes are made to @ARG elements that correspond to actual parameters which were variables, effectively change the values of those variables in the caller, although that change does not occur until control returns to the caller. Consider the following example:

```
sub adder {
    ++$ARG[0];
    ++$ARG[1];
}

$x = 7;
@list = (1, 3, 5);
adder($x, @list);
```

In this example, $x is set to 8 and @list is set to (2 3 5);

The following example again illustrates pass-by-reference parameters:

```
sub interchange {
    ($ARG[1], $ARG[0]) = ($ARG[0], $ARG[1]);
}
...
$a = 7;
$b = 3;
interchange($a, $b);
print "\$a and \$b are now $a and $b \n";
```

produces

```
$a and $b are now 3 and 7
```

The values of the actual parameters, $a and $b, in the call to interchange, are implicitly placed in the @ARG array as its first and second elements. The only statement in interchange uses a list assignment to interchange the first two elements of @ARG. Because $ARG[0] and $ARG[1] are copied back to $a and $b at the point of the function return, this sets $a to 3 and $b to 7.

It is of course silly to attempt to change a literal actual parameter. For example,

```
sub add1 {
    ++$ARG[0];
}

add1(7);
```

does nothing. (It does not even produce an error message.)

6.4.2 PASS-BY-VALUE PARAMETERS

As stated earlier, In Perl, parameters can also be passed by value. To achieve pass-by-value semantics, the values of the actual parameters are often copied from @ARG into my variables in the function. This prevents modification of the actual parameters. For example, consider the following code:

```
sub sub1 {
    my ($x, $y, $z) = @ARG;
    ...
}

...
sub1($a, $b, 7);
```

After this call to sub1, within the body of sub1 during that execution $x, $y, and $z are initialized to the values of $a, $b, and 7, respectively. Regardless of how $x and $y are used in sub1, it does not affect the values of $a and $b in the caller.

The sample function that follows illustrates a pass-by-value parameter. It displays its given integer parameter with its digits in reverse order. For example, if passed 2376, it would display 6732. We use the modulus operator (%) to extract individual digits from the right end of the input parameter, displaying the digits as they are computed. Every time a digit is computed, it is removed from the right end of the remaining number, using division by 10. The terminating condition for the processing loop is that the number becomes less than 1. Because this function uses floating-point arithmetic, it would take a long time to get down to zero, so zero would be a bad choice for the comparison.

```
# reverse_digits (a function)
# Parameters:
#    An integer number
# Return value:
#    None of interest
# Process:
#    Display the given number with its digits in reverse order

use English;
sub reverse_digits {
    my $number = @ARG[0];
    my $digit;
    print "The reverse of $number is: ";

    until ($number < 1) {
        $digit = $number % 10;
        print "$digit";
        $number /= 10;
    }

    print "\n";
}
```

When a hash is passed to a function and pass-by-value semantics are required, the hash is usually the only parameter and the function sets a local hash to the value of @ARG, as in

```
sub sub1 {
    my %my_people = @ARG;
    …
}
…
sub1(%people);
```

The local variable, %my_people, will be assigned all of the elements of @ARG. So, if there were more parameters passed to this function, their values would all end up in %my_people. Perl provides a second method of implementing pass-by-reference parameters, which is described in the next subsection.

6.4.3 PASSING REFERENCES AS PARAMETERS

The second way to implement pass-by-reference parameters, which we prefer in most cases, is to pass references to the actual parameters. The primary advantage of passing a reference over passing the name of an actual parameter variable is most evident when arrays are passed. A reference to an array is a single scalar, whereas passing the name of an array causes all of its elements to be moved to @ARG. Therefore, passing a reference is much faster if the array has significant size. The following samples illustrate passing references to scalars, arrays, and hashes:

For a scalar parameter,

```
sub add_1_scalar {
    my $param = $ARG[0];
    $$param++;
}
...
add_1_scalar(\$sum);
```

For an array,

```
sub add_1_array {
    my $ref_list = $ARG[0];
    my $element;

    foreach $element (@$ref_list) {
        $element++;
    }
}
...
add_1_array(\@list);
```

For a hash,

```
sub add_1_hash {
    my $ref_hash = $ARG[0];
    my $key;

    foreach $key (keys %$ref_hash) {
        $ref_hash -> {$key}++;
    }
}
...
add_1_hash(\%table);
```

Because `shift` uses `@ARG` (or `@_`) as its default operand when used in a function, in each of these cases we could use `shift` instead of `$ARG[0]` to get the actual parameters. (The default operand of `shift` outside function definitions is `@ARGV`; see Chapter 4.)

Consider the following function, which adds 1 to each of its parameters and returns a list of the new values:

```
sub incrementor {
    my @list = @ARG;
    my $element;

    foreach $element (@list) {
        $element++;
    }

    return @list;
}
```

The `incrementor` function could be called with a variety of parameters, as in

```
($count, $sum, @totals) = incrementor($count, $sum, @totals);
```

You must remember, however, that the return value, like the formal parameter `@ARG`, is a single array. So, if you put the array in the target list as the first element, as in the call

```
(@totals, $count, $sum) = incrementor(@totals, $count, $sum);
```

all of the resulting values are returned in `@totals`, and `$count` and `$sum` are set to `undef`.

If you want to call a function and have it get the current version of `@ARG` (the value of `@ARG` before the call), rather than a new one (after the call), it can be done by prefixing the function's name with an ampersand and omitting the parentheses, as in

```
&sub1;
```

6.5   AN EXAMPLE

The next sample function illustrates some of what we have been talking about. Its purpose can be described as follows:

Parameter:
   A hash of names and salaries
Return value:
   An array of the names of those with the top five salaries, in no particular order

For example, for the actual parameter

```
%tst_data = ("Fred" => 200, "Mike" => 240, "Bob" => 220,
             "Darcie" => 190, "Jake" => 195, "Mary" => 215,
             "Louie" => 250, "Betsy" => 175, "Dusty" => 235);
```

the program should output the list

```
Louie
Bob
Mike
Dusty
Mary
```

The approach used in the function, whose name is `top_five`, is as follows: A `while` loop goes over all of the elements of the parameter hash. For each element, another function, `insert_name`, is called, passing the addresses of two arrays, one for the names of those with the top five salaries and one for their salaries, as well as the new name and salary. The first five times it is called, the `insert_name` function simply inserts the given new data into the top five arrays. After that, it finds the lowest salary in the array for the top five salaries. The function compares that lowest salary with the new salary to see if the former should be replaced. When the first function, `top_five`, finds that there are no more data in the given hash, it returns the `top_five` name array.

The code is as follows:

```
# top_five (a function)
# Parameter:
#     A hash of names and salaries
# Return value:
#     An array of the names of those with the top five salaries

use English;

sub top_five {
    my $ref_salaries = $ARG[0];
    my (@top_names, @top_salaries, $name, $salary);

# Go through the input hash and call insert_name with each element

    while (($name, $salary) = each (%$ref_salaries)) {
        insert_name(\@top_names, \@top_salaries, $name, $salary);
    }

    return(@top_names);
} ##- end of function top_five

# insert_name (a function)
# Parameters:
#     The address of an array of names
#     The address of an array of salaries
#     A new name
#     A new salary
# Process: Insert the new name and salary into the arrays, but only
#          if the new salary is higher than the smallest in the given
#          list of five salaries

sub insert_name {
    my($ref_names, $ref_salaries, $new_name, $new_salary) = @ARG;
    my $lowest_salary = 1.0e10;
    my $lowest_salary_index;

# Check to see if there are fewer than five names in the array
#  If not, put the new name and salary into the array

    if (@$ref_names < 5) {
        push @$ref_names, $new_name;
        push @$ref_salaries, $new_salary;

# If the names array already has five names,
#  find the smallest salary in the list

    }else {

        for ($index = 0; $index <= 4; $index++) {
            if ($lowest_salary > $$ref_salaries[$index]) {
                $lowest_salary = $$ref_salaries[$index];
```

```
                    $lowest_salary_index = $index;
           }  ##- end of if ($new_salary >…
     }  ##- end of for ($index,…

# Now compare the current lowest salary with the new salary
# to see if the new salary should replace it
        if ($new_salary > $lowest_salary) {
             $$ref_names[$lowest_salary_index] = $new_name;
             $$ref_salaries[$lowest_salary_index] = $new_salary;
        }  ##- end of if ($new_salary >…

     }  ##- end of else
}  ##- end of function insert_name
```

In some situations, it is convenient to call functions indirectly.

6.6   INDIRECT CALLS TO FUNCTIONS

Suppose that at some point in a program, one of five different functions must be called, depending on the string value of a scalar variable. If functions can be called indirectly, as they can in Perl, we could construct a hash of the possible values of the string and the addresses of the appropriate functions. Then, at the point where the choice must be made, the appropriate function could be called through the value part of the hash element that had the string value as its key.

A function is called indirectly through a variable that has been set to be a reference to a function. A scalar variable can be set to the address of a named function by using the address-of operator (\) and an ampersand (&) on the function's name, as in

```
$ref_fun = \&print_header;
```

This is obviously one of the situations in which the name of the function must be preceded by the ampersand.

Soft references to functions can also be used. A string with the name of the function is assigned to the reference. For example, consider the following statement:

```
$ref_fun_soft = "print_header";
```

Calls to functions through reference variables are the same, whether the reference is soft or hard. Such calls are made by attaching an ampersand to the beginning of the reference's name. Both of the following statements call print_header:

```
&$ref_fun();
&$ref_fun_soft();
```

Perl also supports anonymous functions, which of course must be called through references. An anonymous function can be created by assigning a nameless function definition to a scalar variable. As an example, consider this function:

```
$ref_header = sub {
    print "\n Program Output \n\n";
}
```

Anonymous functions can be called through their reference variables exactly as if they were references to named functions. For the anonymous function previously defined, we could use

```
&$ref_header();
```

6.7 PREDEFINED PERL FUNCTIONS

We have already described some of the predefined Perl functions. There are many more. In this section, we list some of the most commonly used among those we have not already discussed and will not discuss later in the book. Other predefined functions will be described in some detail in later chapters. Complete descriptions of all of them can be found in the `perlfunc` manpage.

abs	Returns the absolute value of its parameter (or $_ if the parameter is omitted).
atan2	Returns the arctangent of the quotient of its two parameters.
chr	Returns the character represented by its numeric parameter.
cos	Returns the cosine of its parameter (which is expressed in radians).
defined	Returns a Boolean value indicating whether the parameter is a defined variable.
eval	Compiles and executes its parameter as if it were a Perl program.
exit	Evaluates its parameter and exits the program with that value.
exp	Returns e to the power of the parameter (if the parameter is omitted, it uses $_).
gmtime	Converts the given time to a Greenwich mean time form.
length	Returns the length in bytes of its parameter expression.
localtime	Returns the value returned by the `time` function as a nine-element list with the time converted to local time.
log	Returns the base-e logarithm of its parameter (if the parameter is omitted, it uses $_).
map	Maps its first parameter (an expression or block), its second parameter (a list) onto each element of and returns a list of the results.
oct	Interprets its parameter as an octal string and returns its value in decimal.
ord	Returns the numeric ASCII value of the first character of its parameter.
rand	Returns a random number between 0 and its parameter's value; if the parameter is omitted, its value is between 0 and 1; the first call to `rand` gets its own initial seed by calling `srand`.
ref	Returns true if its parameter is a reference, false otherwise.
sin	Returns the sine of its parameter, which is expressed in radians (if the parameter is omitted, $_ is used).
sqrt	Returns the square root of its parameters (if the parameter is omitted, $_ is used).

time   Returns the number of nonleap seconds since January 1, 1970.

times   Returns a list of values that specify the time for the current process
                    and the children processes.

vec   Provides a method of packing large numbers of small integer val-
                    ues into a relatively small space.

warn   Produces a message on STDERR, but does not exit.

6.8 THE sort FUNCTION, REVISITED

We introduced the sort function in Chapter 4, but only in its simpler form. That version
uses a string comparison to compare the values being sorted. As we saw in Chapter 4,
this default form of sort does not sort numbers the way we usually want them sorted.

We now describe the more flexible form of call to sort, in which an additional parameter specifies the comparison operation that is to be used in the sort operation. The
new parameter, when it is used, appears as the first parameter. It can take the form of a
function name, a block, or a scalar variable that has either the name or a reference to a
function. In any of these cases, the comparison parameter specifies the code that is to be
used in the comparisons for the sorting process. The comparison process given to sort
must return a number less than zero if the first value being compared belongs before the
second, zero if the order of the two is irrelevant, and a value greater than zero if the
two values must be interchanged. The two values to be compared are referenced in the
comparison code by the names $a and $b. These variables are special, in the sense that
they are exempt from the requirement to be static scoped when use strict 'vars' is
specified. These variables, which act as formal parameters, are used in pass-by-reference
mode. Therefore, they should not be changed in the comparison code.

Perl includes two operators, one for numbers (<=>) and one for strings (cmp). Both
produce 0 if the two operands are equal, 1 if the left operand is greater than the right
operand, and -1 otherwise. The default first parameter to sort is cmp.

This new form of sort can be used on lists of numbers by specifying the <=> operator, as in

```
sort { $a <=> $b; )> @list;
```

If we wanted the array sorted into descending order, we would use

```
sort { $b <=> $a; } @list;
```

Likewise, we can sort lists of strings into reverse alphabetical order by reversing the
order of the references to $a and $b, as in

```
sort { $b cmp $a; } @list;
```

One of the most common uses of the sort function with two parameters is to sort
hashes by their values (rather than their keys). For example, suppose we had a hash
named %top_five that stores the names and salaries of the five highest paid employees
of a company. If we wanted to see this data ordered by the salaries, we could use the following code in the function:

```
print "Employees with the five highest salaries",
      "\nPerson \t Salary \n";
```

```
foreach $key
     (sort { $top_five{$b}> <=> $top_five{$a)>; } keys %top_five) {
     print "$key \t $top_five{$key)> \n";
}
```

As stated earlier, the first parameter to sort could be a function name. For example, we could define a function for the comparison used for %top_five,

```
sub top_five {
    $top_five{$b} <=> $top_five{$a}
}
```

Then the call to sort would be

```
sort top_five keys %top_five;
```

6.9   **THE** pack **AND** unpack **FUNCTIONS**

Occasionally, one encounters or needs files or data structures that are not in the form of text. Hence the need to be able to conveniently convert such files or data structures between text and some binary form. In many cases, the conversion from binary to text can be done with sprintf, which does what printf does, except instead of sending the resulting string to STDOUT, it puts it in the scalar variable specified as sprintf's first parameter. The pack function is a simple alternative to sprintf. The unpack function does the opposite conversion (from text to binary).

Both pack and unpack have the same parameter form, which is a string that contains a conversion format code, and a list that specifies the data to be packed or unpacked. The returned value is the result of the operation. There are a large number of different format codes that can be used in the first parameter. The format code parameter is often called a template. We describe only two of the most commonly used codes here. You can learn about the others in the Perl perlfunc manpage.

The C code specifies an unsigned character value (any unsigned single-byte number). If there are three of these, either CCC or C3 can be specified. When used as a parameter to pack, the C code specifies that each of the given list values be packed into a single byte. All of these bytes are put together in a string. In effect, pack with the C code converts a list of values into a scalar string of ASCII codes. For example, suppose @code_word has the hexadecimal ASCII codes for the letters 'B', 'y', and 'e' (0x42, 0x79, and 0x65). Then

```
$string = pack("C3", @code_word);
```

builds the string "Bye" in $string. When we discuss CGI programming in Chapter 9, we will make use of pack for decoding parameter information sent from an HTML form to a CGI program.

The unpack function does the opposite of pack. In scalar context, it unpacks a single value. In list context, it unpacks a multiple-valued data structure into a list. For example, we could unpack the string we just built with pack by using

```
@code_word = unpack("C3", $string);
```

6.10   SUMMARY

A function definition specifies the name of the function and its actions. A function declaration only specifies that a particular name is that of a function. Perl function definitions are global—they are visible over the whole program file in which they appear. The body of a function, which specifies its actions, is a block. Functions without parameters are normally called with just their names and empty parentheses. A call to a function that has already been defined or declared can omit the parentheses, in which case it has the appearance of a list operator. In a few somewhat rare cases, the name of a function in its call must include an ampersand.

The value of a function is often specified as the parameter in a call to `return`. If no call to `return` is executed before execution reaches the end of a function, the returned value is that of the last expression evaluated. The context of a function call determines the context of the value returned from the function. The context of the call can be determined (by the function) with `wantarray`.

The `my` declaration is used to define variables whose scope and lifetime begin with their definition and end at the end of the block in which they are defined. Such variables, whose primary value is in avoiding name conflicts with names defined outside the function, can be defined in any block, but are most useful in function definitions. Semilocal variables can also be defined with `local`, but these variables have dynamic scoping, making them also visible in called functions. A program can force all variables to be explicitly defined with either `my` or `local` by including a `use strict 'vars'` statement. All variables that are not explicitly defined are globals. (They are visible in the entire file in which they appear.)

Parameters to Perl functions are passed through the global implicit variable `@ARG` (or `@_` if you do not `use English`). References to the actual parameters are implicitly placed in `@ARG`. The function can either use them directly from `@ARG` or explicitly move them to local variables (the most common technique). Whatever the form of the parameters passed to a function, they are forced into the single array, `@ARG`. Pass-by-value semantics are implicit if parameters are moved to local variables. Pass-by-reference semantics are implicit when `@ARG` is used directly. A better way to implement pass-by-reference parameters is to pass references as the actual parameters and move them from `@ARG` to local reference variables in the called function. The syntax of referencing a local hash or array passed this way is to attach a `%` or `@`, respectively, to the front of the name of the local reference.

A reference variable can be set to reference a function, either named or anonymous. Soft references can also be created. Both hard and soft references are used in calls by placing an ampersand and a dollar sign before the first letter of the function's name.

There are a large number of predefined Perl functions; this chapter includes only brief descriptions of some of them and very brief descriptions of a larger subset of them. The `sort` function can include a block to define the comparison operation to be used in the sorting process. This block is specified as the first parameter to `sort`. The `pack` and `unpack` functions are useful for converting the structure of certain kinds of data. Perhaps the most common use of these is to convert data between strings and lists of scalars.

6.11   EXERCISES

Write, test, and debug (if necessary) Perl functions for the following problems:

1. *Parameter:*
   An array of numbers, passed by value.
   Return value:
   The average and median of the parameter array.

2. *Parameter:*
   An array of strings, passed by value.
   Return value:
   A list of the unique strings in the parameter array.

3. *Parameter:*
   A reference to an array of numbers.
   Return value:
   The average and median of the parameter array.

4. *Parameter:*
   A reference to an array of strings.
   Return value:
   A list of the unique strings in the parameter array.

5. *Parameter:*
   A reference to a hash of last names (keys) and first names (values) of famous Olympic sports figures.
   Return value:
   A list in which each element is a string consisting of the name of one of the people in the parameter hash in the form: last name, first name, in alphabetical order.

6. *Parameter:*
   A reference to an array of names in the form: last name, first name, middle initial.
   Return value:
   A hash whose elements consist of the names in the parameter array, where the key is first name and middle initial and the value is the last name.

7. *Parameter:*
   A reference to an array of strings, where each string has the form: first name, middle initial, last name.
   Return value:
   The parameter array, after sorting into alphabetical order based on the last names.

8. *Parameter:*
   A reference to a hash that has numbers as its values.
   Return value:
   An array of the keys of the hash, after sorting them into descending order of the values in the hash.

CHAPTER 7

Pattern Matching

This chapter introduces the powerful but complicated pattern matching capabilities of Perl. We first describe simple patterns and then discuss the more complex patterns, which include anchors, binding operators, or pattern modifiers. Next, we discuss how a part of a string that matches a part of a pattern can be stored and later used, both in and after the pattern. After that, lookahead and lookbehind, which are used to provide context to a match, are introduced. Then we discuss how the `split` function can use general patterns. Finally, the substitute and translate operators are described.

7.1 INTRODUCTION

One of the common programming tasks for system administrators, systems programmers, and application programmers alike is to scan character strings and text files for specific kinds of substrings. This capability is provided by a variety of utilities and software systems. For example, the search and replace operations of editors and word processors, the UNIX `grep` utility, and the `findstr` utility of Windows NT. In addition, compilers, interpreters, and static program analyzers use character patterns to identify lexical and syntactic structures. While some of these needs can be met by separate utilities, it is convenient to have this functionality built in to a programming language, particularly one like Perl, which is frequently used for system administration.

The syntax of Perl's pattern-matching operations is borrowed mainly from the `egrep` UNIX utility. Other UNIX tools that use this sort of pattern matching are the `ed` and `sed` text editors, `awk`, and other members of the `grep` family.

The basis for Perl's pattern matching is the relatively simple regular expressions from theoretical computer science. From that humble beginning, these descriptive mechanisms have grown to become complex and powerful tools for string pattern matching. Indeed, although the pattern matching expressions of Perl are still called regular expressions, they are a far cry from the simple constructs that provided their origin.

In Perl, pattern matching is defined in terms of a single string, but a simple loop can extend any operation on a string to all the strings in a text file. In scalar context, patterns are boolean expressions—they return true or false. They can be specified to remember what part or parts of the string matched part or parts of the pattern. In list context, these matching substrings can be returned in a list. Perl also includes a substitution operator, described in Section 7.7, that replaces matched parts of the string with new strings.

The syntax of a pattern matching operator is

m dl pattern dl [modifiers]

where m is the operator, dl is the character that delimits the pattern, and the modifiers, which are optional, that change how the pattern is used. We delay discussing the modifiers until Section 7.3. The most common delimiter is a slash (/). When slash is used, the m operator is unnecessary. When the slash itself is part of the pattern, such as when you are looking for UNIX paths (e.g., `usr/users/sebesta`), some alternative must be chosen and the m operator must be included, as in

m~pattern~

The delimiter can be any nonalphanumeric, non-white-space character. If you choose (, [, {, or < as the left delimiter, then),], }, or > is the right delimiter, respectively. This will of course be more meaningful after we have introduced patterns.

7.2 SIMPLE PATTERNS

We begin our discussion of patterns with the least complicated patterns, those that simply match individual characters or character classes. A pattern is an abstract representation of a set of strings. A pattern matches when the string with which it is compared is in that set. Patterns range from trivially simple to horrendously complex. The only way to learn to write and understand complicated patterns is to learn about their constituents.

7.2.1 MATCHING CHARACTERS

Characters in patterns fall into three categories: (1) normal characters, which match themselves, (2) metacharacters, which have special meanings in patterns, and (3) the period. Escape sequences, such as \t (tab) and \cC (Control-C), can appear in a pattern, in which case they match themselves. Metacharacters can themselves be matched, but only if they are immediately preceded by a backslash in the pattern. The metacharacters, some of which are special only in certain contexts, are

```
\ | ( ) [ ] { } ^ $ * + ? .
```

While a backslash turns a metacharacter into a normal character, it turns some normal characters into something special. We will discuss these shortly.

The default string to be matched is in $_. In Section 7.3, we discuss how to redirect the pattern matching to a string that is defined with an expression. Consider the following statement:

```
if (/snow/) {
    print "There was snow somewhere in \$_ \n";
}
else {
    print "\$_ was snowless \n";
}
```

In this example, the pattern matcher first scans the contents of $_, left to right, for an s. When an s is found, it checks to see if the next three characters are "now". If they are not, the scan for another s is begun. If the whole pattern is found somewhere in $_, true is returned; otherwise, false is returned. When we are interested only in whether the character pattern matches somewhere in the string and there is actually more than one match in the string, the substring that matched the pattern is irrelevant. In Section 7.3, the position of matching will become relevant, and we will discuss it there.

There is nothing special about a space in a pattern—it is just another normal character to be matched. For example, the pattern

```
/snow days/
```

will only match that exact nine-character string. If there are two spaces between "snow" and "days" in the string, it will not match this pattern.

The period character matches any character except a newline. For example,

```
/a../
```

matches any string that has an a followed by at least two nonnewline characters.

Most patterns have more than one part. A pattern matches a string only if matches are found for all of the parts of the pattern, in order, before the end of the string is reached.

7.2.2 CHARACTER CLASSES

Character classes provide a way to easily specify collections of characters in patterns. A character class is a pattern that is specified as a collection of characters, any one of which can match one character in $_. A character class is defined by placing the characters you want to have in the class in brackets. For example, the pattern

```
/[< >=]/
```

matches any one of the characters <, >, or =. Dashes can be used to specify ranges of characters in a class. For example,

```
/[A-Za-z]/
```

matches any letter. The following pattern matches any octal digit:

```
/[0-7]/
```

If a dash appears at the end of a character class, it is considered a literal dash. For example, the pattern

```
/[0-3-]/
```

matches any of the characters `'0'`, `'1'`, `'2'`, `'3'`, or `'-'`. If you want a literal dash elsewhere in a character class, backslash it.

Sometimes it is convenient to specify a character class by the characters that are not in the class. This can be done by placing a caret character (^) at the left end of the characters, as in

```
/[^A-Za-z]/
```

which matches any nonalphabetic character. The pattern

```
/[^01]/
```

matches any character except 0 or 1.

Some character classes are used sufficiently often to justify predefined abbreviations. These are shown here:

Abbreviation	Equivalent Pattern	Matches
\d	[0-9]	a digit
\D	[^0-9]	a nondigit
\w	[A-Za-z_]	a word character
\W	[^A-Za-z_]	a nonword character
\s	[\r\t\n\f]	a white-space character
\S	[^ \r\t\n\f]	a non-white-space character

Consider the following examples:

/[A-Z]"\s/	matches an uppercase letter, a double quote, and a white-space character
/[\dA-Fa-f]/	matches one hexadecimal digit
/\w\w:\d\d/	matches two word characters, a colon, and two digits

A variable in a pattern of a match operator is interpolated as if the pattern were delimited by double quotes. For example, the following pattern matches a hex digit surrounded by whitespace:

```
$hexpat = "\\s[\dA-Fa-f]\\s";
```

Notice that the \s must be preceded by a backslash to make the other backslash a literal, rather than the 's'. The alternative to the second backslash is to use single quotes to delimit the string. The pattern $hexpat could be used as in the following statement:

```
if (/$hexpat/) {
    print "$_ has a hex digit (or the word 'a') \n";
}
```

7.2.3 QUANTIFIERS

Character and character class patterns can be made more powerful and flexible by adding quantifiers, which allow the patterns to be repeated a specified number of times. Quantifiers, like simple sequences of characters, are considered a form of an operator. Perl has four kinds of quantifiers, specified with *, +, ?, and {m, n}. Quantifiers are specified immediately after a character, character class, or parenthesized subpattern. The most general quantifier has the form of {m, n}, where m and n are numbers. The meanings of these are shown next:

Quantifier	*Meaning*
{n}	exactly n repetitions
{m,}	at least m repetitions
{m, n}	at least m, but not more than n repetitions

Consider the following examples:

/a{1,3}b/	matches ab, aab, and aaab
/ab{3}c/	matches abbbc
/ab{2,}c/	matches abbc, abbbcc, abbbbc, . . .
/(cats){3} z{5}/	matches catscatscats zzzzz
/[abc] {1, 2}/	matches a, b, c, ab, ac, ba, bc, ca, and cb

The other three quantifiers, *, +, and ?, are abbreviations for the more general form, {m, n}. The asterisk quantifier means zero or more repetitions of whatever it quantifies. It is therefore equivalent to {0, }. Consider the following example:

/0\d\d*/	matches an octal literal
/\w\w*/	matches one or more word characters
/bob.*cat/	matches bob and cat separated by zero or more characters, except newline (so, bobcat is a match)

The asterisk quantifier changes the character or class it follows to a pattern that can match the empty string. Prior to this, all patterns we have seen match one or more characters in the string. When an asterisk-quantified pattern matches zero of whatever it quantifies, it matches a position in the string, rather than a character.

Patterns such as \w\w* occur with such frequency that another quantifier, +, is available for them. This quantifier means one or more of whatever it quantifies. It is equivalent to {1, }. For example,

/\w+/	matches one or more word characters
/[A-Za-z][A-Za-z\d_]+/	matches a variable name in a typical programming language
/\d+\.\d+/	matches numbers with a decimal point and at least one digit on each side (Note that it was necessary to backslash the period to prevent it matching just any character)

The question mark quantifier means either zero or one of whatever it quantifies. It is equivalent to {0, 1}. For example,

`/\d+\.?/`	matches a string of at least one digit, possibly followed a decimal point
`/\$?\d+\.\d\d/`	matches a price, with or without the $ (which is backslashed because it is a metacharacter)
`/"?\w+"?/`	matches barewords and words with quotes on either or both sides

Because quantifiers modify the action of a single character or character class, when attached to a string, they modify only the last character. For example, the pattern

```
/ball*/
```

matches `"bal"` followed by zero or more 1's, not zero or more occurrences of the string `"ball"`. Parts of patterns can be grouped with parentheses, allowing a quantifier to apply to whatever is in the parentheses, as in

```
/(ball)*/
```

which matches zero or more occurrences of the string `"ball"`. Also,

```
/(boo! ){3}/
```

matches `"boo! boo! boo! "`.

Note that there is a performance penalty with using these plain parenthesized sub-patterns. This is discussed in Section 7.4.

Consider the following examples:

`/\d{3}-\d{2}-\d{4}/`	matches dashed social security numbers
`/(a ba dee, ){3,4}that's all, folks!/`	matches Porky Pig's sign-off

When braces are used in a context where they can be interpreted as part of a quantifier, they are metasymbols. However, in any other context in a pattern, braces match themselves.

The inclusion of quantifiers in a pattern raises the question of how matches are done when there is more than one substring that matches. First consider the situation of having no quantifier. For example, suppose the value of $_ is `"Tommie"` and the pattern is

```
/m/
```

Which m in `"Tommie"` does this match? To answer the question, you must know the convention of the matching process, which is as follows: Matches are always made at the leftmost position in the string that allows a match of the whole pattern. So, in our example, the left m of the string matches. Assume $_ is still `"Tommie"` and consider the pattern

```
/m*/
```

Now is completely different. In this case, although m and mm would match if the matcher did not try left matches first. The pattern actually matches the empty string, which is, among other places, just before the beginning of the string. That is, the leftmost match is what satisfies the whole pattern. So, although there are two m's in the string, the whole pattern is matched by the empty string, which one can imagine preceding the "T". Of course, the empty string can be imagined to be before any string, after the string, and between any two characters in the string.

Next, consider the pattern

```
/m*i/
```

Now the match (to the same $_ value) is "mmi", because that is the leftmost substring that matches the pattern.

The subpattern .* illustrates the greedy aspect of the pattern matcher. It matches the maximum possible number of nonnewline characters. For example, suppose we have

```
$_ = "Bob sat next to the Bobcat and listened to the Bobolink";
```

Then the pattern

```
/.*Bob/
```

matches the "Bob" in "Bobolink". In effect (but not in fact), the matcher first matches the .* to the whole string, and then backs up one character at a time until it finds a match for the rest of the pattern, "Bob", thereby always finding the rightmost occurrence. The matching process operates the same way for all quantified patterns.

As another example, consider

```
$_ = "Freddie's hot dogs";
/Fred+/
```

This results in a match of "Fredd". The matcher begins this operation by matching the first three characters of the string, 'F', 'r', and 'e'. Then it matches 'd+' in the pattern to all following consecutive d's in the string, in this example just 'dd'. The matcher matches 'd's in the pattern to characters in the string until it fails.

The matcher can deal with quantifiers in two nearly opposite modes, greedy, which is the default and is illustrated in the previous exammple, and minimal. The minimal mode is specified by following the quantifier with a question mark. For example, in

```
$_ = "Freddie's hot dogs";
/Fred+?/
```

the match is "Fred". In this case, the minimal version of the pattern is "Fred", so the matcher need not look further into the string.

As another example, consider

```
$_ = "Freddie's hot hogs are really hot!";
/.*hot/
```

In this example, which is once again the greedy mode, the matcher tries as many characters for the .* part as possible (in this case, the length of the string). If that does not match, and of course it cannot here, the matcher tries one fewer characters for that part, and so forth, until it matches the last occurrence of "hot". On the other hand, in

```
$_ = "Freddie's hot dogs are really hot!";
/.*?hot/
```

the match is of the left occurrence of `"hot"`, because it tries first with no characters for `.*?`, and then tries one character, and so forth, until the other part of the pattern matches, thereby finding the first `"hot"`.

The last question concerning matching quantified subpatterns is what happens if you have two quantified subpatterns in a pattern. For example, suppose we have

```
$_ = "Bob sat next to the Bobcat and listened to the Bobolink";
/Bob.*Bob.*link/
```

In this case, the first `.*` matches

```
" sat next to the Bobcat and listened to the "
```

even though it could also match

```
" sat next to the ";
```

which is left of the first option. The rule for a pattern with two quantified subpatterns is that the leftmost of them is greediest.

The alternation operator is used in patterns to specify alternative subpatterns.

7.2.4 ALTERNATION

Alternation, specified with a vertical bar (|), is a pattern operator. As is usually the case in programming languages, the vertical bar symbolizes the logical OR operator in a pattern. For example, one could have

```
/a|e|i|o|u/
```

which means the same as

```
/[aeiou]/
```

but requires more typing. However, alternation can also be used between strings, as in

```
/Fred|Mike|Dracula/
```

Parentheses may be used to group alternatives, as in

```
/(Bob|Tom|Pussy|Scaredy)cat/      matches Bobcat, Tomcat, . . .
/t(oo?|wo)/                       matches to, too, and two
```

The pattern matcher attempts to match the alternatives left to right. Therefore, the pattern

```
/Tom|Tommie/
```

never matches `"Tommie"`.
In the pattern

```
/\d+\.?\d*|\.\d+/
```

the first alternative matches strings of one or more digits, possibly followed by a decimal point and more digits. The second alternative matches a decimal point, followed by one or more digits. So, this pattern matches numeric literals without exponents.

It is not necessary to use alternation in a character class, because it is already implicit there. In fact, if alternation is used in a character class, it almost always means something different from what was intended. For example, the character class

```
[belly|belts|bells]
```

is equivalent to

```
[belyts]
```

because all of the characters from the three strings are simply put together to form the character class.

To correctly write a pattern that includes more than one pattern operator, you must know the order of evaluation of those operators.

7.2.5 PRECEDENCE OF THE PATTERN OPERATORS

We have now discussed several pattern operators. As with other kinds of expressions, to understand pattern expressions one must know the precedence of pattern operators, which dictate the order of their evaluation by the pattern matcher. The precedence of the operators discussed so far is

parentheses	highest
quantifiers	
character sequence	
alternation	lowest

Therefore, the pattern

```
/#|-+/
```

matches either a single pound sign or one or more dashes, rather than one or more occurrences of either a pound sign or a dash. If this latter interpretation is desired, it can be had by including parentheses at the appropriate spots, as in

```
/(#|-)+/
```

7.3   MORE COMPLEX PATTERNS

So far we have discussed only relatively simple patterns. More complicated patterns can be designed by including anchors and pattern modifiers. The actions of the pattern matcher can be partially controlled by including anchor operators in the pattern. Pattern modifiers change the way in which the matcher operates with the modified pattern.

7.3.1 ANCHORS

An anchor in a pattern requires that a part of the pattern match at specific kinds of places in the string. This allows the alignment of a particular position in the pattern with a particular position in the string. The simplest anchors are those that require that the pattern match at the beginning (^) or end ($) of the string. For example,

```
/^Shelley/
```

matches `"Shelley has red hair"`, but not `"What color is Shelley's hair?"`. Likewise,

```
/hair$/
```

matches the first string, but not the second (because the second string has a question mark between `"hair"` and the end of the string). The caret character (^) matches itself if it appears anywhere in a pattern, except at the left end or inside a character class. If you want a caret to match at the beginning of a string, backslash it. The three uses of the caret are illustrated in the pattern

```
/^[^!]^/
```

which matches any string that does not begin with `!`, but has a caret as its second character.

Anchor operators in patterns do not match characters in the string; rather, they match positions between characters in the string. Because of this, anchor operators are sometimes called assertions. For example, the ^ at the beginning of a pattern does not match any characters in the string. When such a pattern matches, the caret matches the position just before the first character of the string.

The \b anchor matches the position between a word character (\w) and a non-word character (\W). This can be used on both sides of a word pattern to match a string that is not embedded in another word. For example,

```
/\bwear\b/
```

matches `"I wear old shoes"`, but not `"Swimwear for sale"` or `"Molly wears green sweaters"`.

Perl includes some other anchor operators, but because they are less often useful, we do not discuss them in this book.

It is not always convenient to match the string in `$_`. Binding operators provide a way to match other strings.

7.3.2 BINDING OPERATORS

Perl allows a pattern to be matched against any string by connecting that string to the pattern with one of the binding operators, `=~` or `!~`. For example,

```
$string =~ /[,;:]/
```

tries to find a comma, semicolon, or colon in `$string`.

```
$string !~ /[,;:]/
```

does exactly the same pattern matching as the preceding expression, but it inverts the logic of the returned value. Therefore, this pattern returns true only if the search for a comma, semicolon, or colon in `$string` fails. The binding operators are actually Boolean operators, for they return Boolean values.

The left operand of the binding operators can be any expression that yields a string value. When used in scalar context, the input operator yields a string value. Therefore, it can be used as the left operand of a binding operator. As an example, consider the following statement:

```
if (<STDIN> =~ /^[Yy]/) { ... }
```

Because the `=~` and `!~` operators have high precedence, when an expression is used as the left operand, it must be parenthesized.

In many cases, it is convenient to be able to specify some special handling of a pattern by the matcher.

7.3.3 PATTERN MODIFIERS

A pattern may be followed by a modifier, which either changes how the pattern is interpreted or how the pattern matcher works while using the pattern. The `i` modifier tells the pattern matcher to ignore the case of letters in the string. For example,

```
/apples/i
```

matches `"apples"`, `"Apples"`, `"APPLES"`, `"ApLlEs"`, and every other combination of uppercase and lowercase letters that spell the plural of that fruit.

The `if` statement that tests for inputs that begin with an uppercase or lowercase `y` in Section 7.3.2 can be rewritten as

```
if (<STDIN> =~ /^y/i) { ... }
```

The `m` modifier specifies that the string is to be treated as multiple lines, assuming it has embedded newlines. This causes `^` to match just after any newline in the string. Likewise, `$` matches just before any newline in the string.

The `s` modifier specifies that the string is to be treated as a single line, which changes the period character, so that in patterns it also matches the newline character. This is used when the entire string is to be considered a single line, regardless of embedded newline characters.

If both the `s` and `m` modifiers are specified, a period in the pattern matches any character in the string, including newline. However, `^` and `$` match the position just before and just after a newline, respectively.

Patterns may include scalar variables. When they do, the variables are interpolated, just as if they appeared in a quoted string literal. Every time such a pattern is used, it is recompiled, just in case the value of the variable has changed. This provides dynamic patterns, but they are expensive to use. If a pattern includes a scalar variable, but the value of that variable never changes during the different times the pattern is used, the `o` modifier should be included on the pattern. This modifier tells `perl` to not recompile the pattern during execution of the program.

The `x` modifier allows the inclusion of white space between the parts of a pattern without changing what the pattern matches. For example,

```
/\d+ \. \d+/x
```

is equivalent to

```
/\d+\.\d+/
```

Comments count as white space, so they can also be included in patterns that include the `x` modifier. This is especially useful for long and complex patterns, for it allows the separate parts to appear on separate lines and every line can include a comment that explains what kinds of things it matches. For example, consider the following pattern:

```
/\d+ # The digits before the decimal point
 \.             # The decimal point
 \d+            # The digits after the decimal point
 /x
```

Parts of a string that matches parts of a pattern can be "remembered," allowing it to be used in later parts of the pattern, or even after the pattern.

7.4   REMEMBERING MATCHES

In some cases, we want to be able to reference the part of the string that matched the pattern, right in the pattern. This is made possible by parenthesizing the part of the pattern that is of interest. The part of the string that matched can be referenced in the pattern through implicitly defined variables. The part of the string that matched the first parenthesized part of the pattern is in \1. The part that matched the second parenthesized part, if there is one, is in \2, and so forth. For example,

```
/(\w+).*\1/
```

matches strings like "jo likes joanne" and "Duran Duran". Likewise,

```
/(.)\1/
```

matches the first double character it finds, for example the "oo" in "I like football!".

If the parts of the string that matched the parenthesized parts of the pattern are needed outside the pattern, the variables $1, $2, and so forth are used instead of \1, \2, and so forth. For example,

```
"TD ran for 305 yards today" =~ /(\d+) (\w+) (\w+)/;
print "$1 $2 $3 \n";
```

displays

```
305 yards today
```

If there are nested parentheses in a pattern, they are related to the matching variables by counting left parentheses from the left end of the pattern. For example, the code:

```
$_ = "17 May 1998";
/((\d+) (\w+) (\d+))/;
print "$1 \n $2 $3 $4 \n";
```

displays

```
17 May 1998
17 May 1998
```

As a simple example of a situation where minimal quantified matching is needed, consider the task of matching a literal character string. The end of the literal string is the first occurrence of whatever quote appeared at the beginning. Therefore, the following pattern will work:

```
/(['"])(.*?)\1/
```

After the matching process, the literal string is in $2. Without the minimal match for .*, this pattern would match the literal string from the first quote to the last quote character (rather than the first one found).

In a list context, a pattern operator returns a list of the values of $1, $2, and so forth. So,

```
$_ = "17 May 1998";
($day, $month, $year) = /(\d+) (\w+) (\d+)/;
```

does the right thing, although `split` would have been better for this.

The \n and $n implicit variables are called backreferences, because they refer to the results of previous matches. If a pattern includes at least one ordinary parenthesized subpattern, all of the backreference variables are reset. If a pattern has no ordinary parentheses, the backreference variables retain their previous values.

Perl includes three implicit variables, $`, $&, and $', that can be used to reference the part of the string before the match, the part that matched, and the part after the match, respectively. If you use `English`, the names are $PREMATCH, $MATCH, and $POSTMATCH.

Note that in terms of performance it is costly for the matcher to save these three substrings after every pattern match. If none of these three implicit variables appear in your program, `perl` will not bother saving the substrings. If just one of the variables appears somewhere, all matches are required to save the three substrings.

Perl's regular expressions allow the context of a substring to be used to specify a match to a pattern.

7.5   EXTENSIONS TO REGULAR EXPRESSIONS

Perl includes several extensions to previous versions of its regular expression syntax that are defined within parentheses in a pattern. The general form of these extensions is

(?xPattern)

where x is a one- or two-character code that defines the specific extension. The following subsections describe some of the most commonly used extensions.

7.5.1 NONBACKREFERENCING PARENTHESES

It is often convenient to be able to group parts of a pattern by using parentheses. If you are going to use backreferencing to the parts of the string that matched the parenthesized part, this is fine. If you are not going to use backreferencing, these parentheses unncessarily slow the matching process. In this case, the ' : ' extension can be used, which specifies that the parentheses do not provide backreferencing, thereby saving the time the matcher would use saving matched substrings. For example,

```
/(?:Bob|Tom|Pussy|Scaredy)cat/
```

is more efficient than the version we presented in Section 7.2.4.

7.5.2 LOOKAHEADS

Sometimes we need to specify a pattern that only matches if it is followed immediately by something, but we do not want the following substring to be part of the match. This is useful when we save the matched substring and also when the next part of the pattern must match something immediately after the current match. These are called *zero-width positive lookaheads*. They are specified by the ' = ' extension. For example, the pattern

```
/\d+(?=\.)/
```

matches a string of digits followed immediately by a decimal point, but does not include the decimal point in $MATCH and also leaves it in the string if the matcher finds subsequent matches in the same pattern.

The lookahead can also be specified to be negative, meaning that we want a match only if the subpattern is not followed by some particular thing. These are called *zero-width negative lookaheads*. They are specified by the `'!'` extension. For example,

```
/\d+(?!\.)/
```

matches a string of digits that is not followed immediately by a decimal point.

7.5.3 LOOKBEHINDS

Perl also allows zero-width lookbehinds, which behave similarly to the zero-width lookaheads. `'<='` specifies a positive lookbehind; `'<!'` specifies a negative lookbehind. For example,

```
/(?<=\.)d+/
```

matches a string of digits that is immediately preceded by a decimal point, and

```
/(?<!\.)d+/
```

matches a string of digits that is *not* immediately preceded by a decimal point.

The next section describes how general patterns can be used with the split function.

7.6   THE split FUNCTION, REVISITED

Recall that we discussed the split function in Chapter 4, at which time, we used only empty strings or single characters for the Pattern parameter, as in

```
@names = split /,/, "Betty,Bert,Bart,Bartholomew";
```

that sets @names to "Betty", "Bert", "Bart", "Bartholomew",. The first parameter to split can be any pattern. So, if the string of names had blanks after the commas, we could deal with that with

```
@names = split /, /, "Betty, Bert, Bart, Bartholomew";
```

which results in the same value for @names as the previous example. Or, suppose that the names were separated by digits surrounded by colons, as in

```
"Betty:778:Bert:2222:Bart:43297:Bartholomew"
```

then the pattern

```
/:\d+:/
```

would do the job in this case.

If we want to parse words that are separated by whitespace, we could use

```
/\s+/
```

as the first parameter to split.

7.7 SUBSTITUTIONS

It is common to need to find a particular substring in a string and replace it with a different substring. Perl provides a powerful operator for this process: the substitution operator. This operator uses the patterns discussed in the previous parts of this chapter to replace parts of strings that matched. The general form of the substitution operator is

    s dl Pattern dl New_string dl Modifiers

where the dl's are delimiters. In its most common form, without modifiers, it looks like

    s/Pattern/New_string/

As with the match operator, if slash clashes with something in either Pattern or New_string, the delimiter can be set to whatever you like. Both Pattern and New_string are treated like quoted strings in the sense that any scalar variables that appear in them are interpolated. This interpolation in the Pattern occurs just once, when the operator is evaluated. Interpolation in the New_string occurs every time there is a match. (The use of the g modifier, explained next, allows for multiple matches.) Of course, if you choose apostrophes as the delimiter, that would stifle the interpolation of any variables appearing in either Pattern or New_string. Consider the following examples:

```
$_ = "No more apples!";
s/apples/applets/;        # Changes $_ to "No more applets!"

$_ = "Who are Jack & Jill?";
s/(\w+) & (\w+)/$2 & $1/;
# Changes $_ to "Who are Jill & Jack?"
```

If the substitute operator is used with a binding operator (=~ or !~), the left operand must have an l-value.

The substitution operator is made more flexible with the use of one or more of the available modifiers. We now discuss only the most commonly used substitution operators. The i, o, m, and x modifiers have the same effect with the substitution operator as they do with the match operator. The g modifier tells perl to carry out the substitution everywhere in the string that the pattern matches. Consider the following examples:

```
s/ +/ /g                  # Reduces all multiple spaces to single spaces
$_ = "12034005";
s/0//g;                   # Changes $_ to "12345"

s/mispelled/misspelled/g  # Fixes all misspellings in $_
$_ = "Molly and Mary were molls";
s/(\w+)/"\1"/g;
# Now $_ is '"Molly" "and" "Mary" "were" "molls"'

$_ = "Is it Sum, SUM, sum, or suM?";
s/sum/sum/ig;
# Now $_ is "Is it sum, sum, sum, or sum?"
```

The returned value of the substitution operator is the number of replacements that were made, or the value is false if none were made. Of course, there can only be more than one if the g modifier is used.

The e modifier can be specified in a substitution, but its meaning in that context has no connection to its meaning with a match operator. Rather, it specifies that the

New_string part of the substitute is to be treated as a Perl expression and interpreted to produce the value to be substituted. There is an example of the use of this modifier in Section 7.8.

7.8 AN EXAMPLE

This example is a program to modify the text given in a file. Assume that the file was constructed long ago, and because of that, it used a very limited character set, specifically, that of FORTRAN IV, which provided only 48 characters. Our only interest here is that the character set had only uppercase letters and did not include semicolons, exclamation points, double quotes, or question marks. In our text file to be processed, these four special characters are coded as two-digit numbers prefixed with colons. Specifically, :10 represents a semicolon, :11 represents an exclamation point, :12 represents a double quote, and :13 represents a question mark.

There are two different processes that must be performed on the file: First, the character codings must be converted to the characters they represent. This can be done with a global substitution operator. The second process is more complicated. We must convert most of the uppercase letters in the file to lowercase. Converting them all to lowercase is easily done with the lc operator. After that, we must convert the first letter of each sentence to uppercase. Also, we must convert all occurrences of the personal pronoun I to uppercase. There may be other situations where a letter must be converted to uppercase, but these are the only conversions we will consider here.

Because we must be able to find the beginning characters of sentences—and sentences can span lines in the file—it is most convenient to treat the whole file as one string. It is one of the great strengths of Perl that we can conveniently do this (since strings have no length limit, other than the size of your computer's memory). We can make a single line input operator read the entire file into a scalar variable by changing the input file separator to a character that does not appear in the file. That makes the operator think the whole file is a single string. This can be done by setting the implicit variable in which the input line separator is stored, $/, to the octal number 777, which is not the code of any ASCII character.

If the first non-white-space character of the file is a letter, it obviously must be converted to uppercase. If the file is in the variable $file, this can be done with

```
$file =~ s/\s*(^[a-z])/uc($1)/e;
```

Notice that we included the e modifier, because the uc operator in the new string part of the substitution must be executed.

Next, we must find the first letter of each sentence and convert it to uppercase. The beginning of a sentence can be found by first finding the end of the previous sentence. Sentences end in periods, exclamation points, and question marks. So, when we find one of those, we skip the white space, and convert the next letter to uppercase. Since this operation must be done to the whole file, the g modifier must be included, along with the e to execute the lc character conversion and the m modifier to specify that the substitute operator must treat the string as multiple lines. The conversion can be done with

```
$file =~ s/([.!\?])(\s+)([a-z])/$1 . $2 . uc($3)/gem;
```

We have ignored several possibilities here. For example, if a quoted phrase happens to be a complete sentence, its first letter must be capitalized.

Finally, we must find the occurrences of the personal pronoun, I, and convert them to uppercase. We assume that any letter i that is preceded and followed by a space is a personal pronoun. The conversion is done with the simple statement

```
$file =~ s/ i / I /g;
```

Following is the program that puts all of this together to do the reformatting process we just described:

```
# formatter
#     Input:   A file of text, specified on the command line
#     Output:  A listing of the file, after the following modifications
#               1. All occurrences of :10 converted to semicolons
#               2. All occurrences of :11 converted to exclamation points
#               2. All occurrences of :12 converted to double quotes
#               3. All occurrences of :13 converted to question marks
#               4. All letters converted to lowercase, except the first letter
#                  of each sentence (sentences end in ., !, or ?) and i's that
#                  are preceded and followed by a space

# Get the whole file with <> by first setting the input record
# separator to an invalid character

$/ = 0777;
$file = <>;

# Do the coded character conversions

$file =~ s/:10/;/g;
$file =~ s/:11/!/g;
$file =~ s/:12/"/g;
$file =~ s/:13/?/g;

# Convert all letters in the file to lowercase

$file = lc $file;

# If the first nonwhite space character of the file is a letter,
# convert it to uppercase

$file =~ s/\s*([a-z])/uc($1)/e;

# Find the first letter following each sentence terminator and
# convert it to uppercase

$file =~ s/([.!\?])(\s+)([a-z])/$1 . $2 . uc($3)/gem;

# If there are any lowercase is followed by a space,
# convert them to uppercase

$file =~ s/ i / I /g;

print "The fixed file is: \n\n$file \n";
```

7.9   TRANSLATING CHARACTERS

In some situations, we want a substitution operation to be based on characters, rather than strings. When this is the case, the translate operator is used. The translate operator, `tr`, does not use patterns, so it is somewhat tenuous how this operator fits into this chapter. However, its appearance is certainly similar to that of a substitution operator; hence, it will be described here. The general form for the translate operator is

> tr/Search_List/Replacement_List/

Search_List and Replacement_List are specifications of characters (not patterns or strings). When translate finds a character in the string that matches one in Search_List, it replaces the character in the string with the character at the corresponding position in Replacement_List. The translate operator returns the number of characters from Search_List it found in the string. Consider the following examples:

```
tr/a-z/A-Z/;      # Translates all lowercase letters in $_ to
                  # uppercase
tr/\./\./;        # Returns the number of periods in $_, but
                  # does not change it
tr/://;           # Erases all colons in $_
```

The translate operator, like the match operator, can employ the binding operators to apply itself to any specified string.

There are several modifiers that can be specified on a translate operation, but they are rarely useful. It is worth noting, however, that there is no `o` modifier, such as that of the match operator. The reason for this is that neither Search_List nor Replacement_List interpolate embedded variables.

7.10   SUMMARY

The most common form of the pattern match operator uses slashes as delimiters and does not include the `m` operator. When the slash is inconvenient, another character is used and the `m` does appear. Simple patterns consist of characters, which match themselves; metacharacters, which have special meaning in patterns; and periods, which match any character except newline. A character class specifies a collection of characters, any one of which can be used for the match. Within a class, dashes can be used to specify ranges of characters. A caret at the beginning of a character class means all characters except those in the class. Some character classes have abbreviations. For example, \d means any digit, \w means any word character, and \s means any white-space character.

Three different quantifiers can follow any character or character class in a pattern, *, +, and {m, n}. These mean zero or more, one or more, and at least m but not more than n repetitions of whatever they follow, respectively. Quantifiers can also follow parenthesized groupings of characters.

The default operation of the pattern matcher is that it finds the leftmost substring that matches the whole pattern. If a quantifier is involved, the quantified pattern matches the maximum number of repetitions that result in a match. If you want quantifiers to match the minimum number of repetitions, attach a question mark to the quantifier. A pattern can include alternation operators, which separate alternative patterns. The alternative patterns are tried left to right until a match is found or all possibilities have been tried without success. The precedence of pattern operators, from highest to lowest, is as follows: parentheses, quantifiers, character sequence, and alternation.

Patterns can be anchored at the left or right end of the string or at a word/nonword boundary with ^, $, and \b, respectively. A string, specified as an expression with either an l-value or an r-value, can be the target of a pattern match by binding the expression to the pattern with either =~ or !~. The !~ operator simply inverts the logic of the value of the match. Patterns can be modified with i, which specifies case-insensitive matching of letters; m, which specifies that the string is to be treated as multiple lines; s, which specifies the period also matches the newline characters; o, which specifies that the pattern is not to be recompiled in uses after the first; and x, which specifies that white space and comments in the pattern are to be ignored by the matcher.

Parentheses in patterns have the side effect of setting implicit variables to the substrings of the string that it matched. The match of the leftmost parenthesized subpattern is put in \1, the match of the second parenthesized subpattern from the left is put in \2, and so forth. If the matching substrings are needed outside the pattern, the corresponding implicit variables $1, $2, and so forth can be used.

Perl defines several extensions to regular expressions, which are specified in parenthesized subpatterns. These are ':', which prevents parentheses from forcing the matcher to remember matched parts of the string; lookaheads ('=' and '!') and lookbehinds ('<=' and '<!'), which allow patterns to specify required context on one end or the other of the matched part of the string.

The split function can use any pattern as its first parameter. The substitution operator uses a pattern to find substrings and a second parameter as the new substring that is to replace the matched substring. The g modifier can be used to specify that all matches in the string are to be replaced. The e modifier tells perl to treat the second parameter as an expression to be compiled and executed. The translate operator is used to translate specific characters to other specific characters. It is often used to count the number of a particular character or class of characters in the string.

7.11   EXERCISES

Write and debug if necessary Perl programs for the following problems:

1. Input: A file specified on the command line that contains text.

    Output: The input text after the following modifications have been made:
    1. All multiple spaces are reduced to single spaces.
    2. All occurrences of Darcy are replaced with Darcie.
    3. All lines that begin with ~ are deleted.
    4. All occurrences of 1998 are replaced with 1999.

2. Input: A file specified on the command line that contains a C program.

    Output: For each line of the input,
    1. The number of words (variables and reserved words) on the line.
    2. The number of numeric literals without decimal points on the line.
    3. The number of numeric literals with decimal points on the line.
    4. The number of braces and parentheses on the line.

3. Input: A file specified on the command line that contains text.

   Output: The input text after the following modifications have been made:

   1. The first letter of the first word on each line must be converted to uppercase.
   2. All numbers that end lines must have a decimal point attached.
   3. All semicolons must be replaced by commas.

4. Input: A file specified on the command line that contains text.

   Output: All lines in the input that contain all of the four digits, 2, 4, 6, and 8, in any order.

5. Input: A file specified on the command line that contains text.

   Output: All lines in the input that contain all of the four digits, 2, 4, 6, and 8, in order. These digits can be separated by zero or more of any other characters.

6. Input: A file specified on the command line that contains a C program.

   Output: The lines of the input file with all comments deleted (C comments have the form `/* ... */`).

7. Input: A file specified on the command line that contains a Perl program.

   Output: The lines of the input file with all comments deleted.

8. Input: A file specified on the command line that contains text.

   Output: The lines in the input file with all white space deleted.

CHAPTER 8

Files, Input and Output, and Formats

In the earlier chapters, we discussed how external files can be read in Perl using command-line arguments. This chapter introduces a more general and conventional approach to reading and writing files. Although opening, closing, reading, and writing files in Perl is closely related to those operations in other languages, Perl includes some very different input and output capabilities. Among these are operators that return file parameters, functions for deleting and renaming files, and a facility for producing formatted reports.

8.1   FILEHANDLES AND FILES

A file is a sequence of bytes of text or data, which is usually stored on a disk. Perl, like most languages and systems that originated in the UNIX environment, has three pre-defined files, one for keyboard input, one for screen output, and one for error messages (which is also usually directed to the screen). All files are referenced in Perl programs through special Perl variables called *filehandles*. Once the connection between a file-handle and an actual file has been established in a program, the file is referenced through the filehandle. This connection is specified with open and destroyed with close, which are described later in this section.

   Names of filehandles do not begin with a special character—they are bare word names. This is rarely a problem, because the context of a filehandle usually clarifies its name space. To insure no conflicts with present or future reserved words, by convention filehandles are spelled with all uppercase letters. We have already seen this with STDIN, STDOUT, and STDERR, the filehandles for the three predefined Perl files.

Before discussing reading and writing files, we introduce the functions for opening and closing files.

8.2   OPENING AND CLOSING FILES

open is the function (or list operator) that specifies the connection between a file and a filehandle. Its function call format is

    open(filehandle, filename)

where the filename can be specified with a string expression or a simple string literal. If the file being opened is to be used for anything except reading, its filename in the open must be preceded by one or two special characters that specify the file's use. The most commonly used among these are shown here:

Character(s)	Meaning
>	Output, starting at the beginning of the file (overwriting the previous contents)
>>	Output, starting at the end of the current data in the file
<	Input (the default)

For example,

```
open(INDAT, "scores");
open(RESULTS, ">grades");
```

The first call to open connects the filehandle INDAT with the file named scores and opens it for input. The second call to open connects the filehandle RESULTS with the file named grades and opens it for output, starting at its beginning (which destroys anything previously written to the file).

The open function can fail for several different reasons; for example, if an attempt is made to open a file for input that does not exist, open returns true if it succeeds and false if it fails. The Perl idiom for checking whether open succeeded or not is to use an or operator and a die function with the open. For example, consider the following statement

```
open(INDAT, "scores") or die "Error--unable to open scores $!";
```

As discussed in Chapter 3, die displays its operand and terminates the program. If a newline is included in the die operand, no additional information is included. However, if the newline is not included, as in the previous example, Perl attaches the file name of the program and the line number of the open in the program that failed. Recall that $! has an error diagnostic message from the system.

Opened files are always closed implicitly just before they are reopened (with a subsequent open function call) and when the program terminates. However, some programmers prefer to explicitly close their files. This can be done with the close function, as in

```
close(RESULTS) or die "Error--unable to close grades$!";
```

The call to `die` is included because it is possible for `close` to fail. An example of a `close` failure would be if there was not enough disk space to write the buffer contents to the file. (Buffer contents are written to disk when a file that was opened for writing is closed.)

The `open` function can also be used to open mechanisms that are not files, such as pipes. Pipes are discussed briefly in Chapter 10, after we introduce techniques for launching processes.

8.3   READING AND WRITING FILES

As you will see, file reading and writing are simple operations in Perl. Any text file can be read and written one line at a time. Files can also be read multiple lines at a time.

8.3.1   READING AND WRITING ONE LINE

We have read and written single lines of text files (from the keyboard and to the screen) in nearly all of the examples in this book, so doing it with other files that are opened in our programs is not really new. Reading a line from a file other than STDIN is just a matter of substituting the file's filehandle for STDIN in the input line operator, <>. Writing a line to a file opened in the program is done by using `print`, with the filehandle as the first parameter, as in

```
print RESULTS "Sum = $sum \n";
```

Notice that the file name in this statement is not followed by a comma.

The example that follows illustrates opening, reading, writing, and closing simple text files. It reads lines from a file, each of which stores a name. It displays the lines that have first names that have endings that makes them sound as if they were children's names.

```
# new_file
# Input:  A file named names, whose lines have the form
#             Lastname, Firstname, MiddleInitial
# Output: A new file named kids, which has the lines from the input
#             file whose first names end in ie, y, or i.

open(ALLNAMES, "names") or die "Error--cannot open names $!";
open(KIDDIES, ">kids") or die "Error--cannot open kids $!";

# Loop to get a name and display it if it is that of a kid

while (<ALLNAMES>) {
    if (/,.*(ie,|y,|i,)/) { print KIDDIES; }  ## Two uses of $_
}

close(ALLNAMES) or die "Error--cannot close names $!";
close(KIDDIES) or die "Error--cannot close kids $!";
```

The pattern used in this program looks for words that appear between commas, which are first names, that end in `"ie"`, `"y"`, or `"i"`.

8.3.2 READING MORE THAN ONE LINE

The read function is used to read segments longer than one line from a file. On long files, this can lower the number of read operations and hasten execution of the program. The data read by read goes into a program scalar variable, which serves as a buffer. The form of a call to read is

```
read(filehandle, buffer, length [, offset]);
```

where the brackets mean that what is between them is optional. The buffer parameter is the scalar variable into which input is read, length is the number of bytes this read is meant to read, and the optional offset is a position in the buffer where you want the characters that were read to go. If omitted, the offset is zero. The read function returns the number of bytes it actually read into the buffer. It returns zero when the file is at its end and no characters can be read. It returns undef if an error occurs during the read operation.

The following sample program that follows illustrates the read function on an input file similar to that for the new_file program. In this case, the lines are 19 characters long, 20 counting the newline. The program reads three of these lines at a time and displays those that are names of kids, as defined in its initial documentation.

```
# new_file_read

# Input:  A file named names, whose lines have the form
#              Lastname, Firstname, MiddleInitial
#              Each line is 19 characters long, not counting the newline
# Output: A new file named kiddies, which has the lines from the input
#              file whose first names end in ie, y, or i.
# Method: This program must use read to read three lines at a time

open(ALLNAMES, "names") or die "Error--cannot open names $!";
open(KIDDIES, ">kids") or die "Error--cannot open kids $!";

# Read the first three lines

$return = read(ALLNAMES, $buf, 60);

# Loop to process three lines

while ($return) {
    @lines = split /\n/, $buf;

    foreach $line (@lines) {

# If it is a kid, write it and a newline to the kids file

        if ($line = ~ /,.*(ie,|y,|i,)/) {
            print KIDDIES $line . "\n";
        } ##- end of if
    } ##- end of foreach loop

# Read three more lines

    $return = read(ALLNAMES, $buf, 60);
} ##- end of while loop
```

```
close(ALLNAMES) or die "Error--cannot close names $!";
close(KIDDIES) or die "Error--cannot close kids $!";
```

8.4 PORTABILITY AND FILES

Perl programs that must run on different systems can have problems with file and path names. Path names and file names can be a problem if you attempt to write a portable Perl program or a portable program in any other language, for that matter. File names for DOS systems are limited to eight characters plus a three-character extension, with no embedded blanks. For Windows 95, 98, and NT, file names can be much longer and can have embedded blanks. Perl cannot deal with file names with embedded blanks. Also, in the Microsoft operating systems, file names are not case sensitive, but in UNIX they are. So, there are several different reasons why it is sometimes difficult to use path or file names in a program that will be valid on all possible platforms.

Although UNIX uses slash characters to separate path name components and DOS and Windows 95 use backslashes, Perl recognizes both so it is not a problem. However, because backslash is used in Perl as an escape character, you must write two backslashes to get one.

8.5 FILE TESTS

Because there are situations in which your program needs to know something about a file before it uses it, Perl's file test operators allow a program to determine a file's characteristics before performing any operations on the file. For example, suppose your program creates a new file by opening it for writing, but there is some possibility that a file with the same name already exists, but has some entirely different use. It is convenient to check for such a file before you open and use it for your purposes, because your new program is about to destroy whatever is currently stored under that file name. Perl includes a collection of file tests that provide vital information about existing files. File tests are unary operators whose operand is an expression that evaluates to a string, which is either a file name or a filehandle. Most, but not, all file tests return true or false. The form of the file test operators is similar to that of UNIX shell command flags: a minus sign and a single letter. The most commonly used file tests are shown here:

File Test	Returns
-e	True if the file exists
-r	True if the file is readable
-w	True if the file is writable
-x	True if the file is executable
-d	True if the file is a directory
-f	True if the file is a regular file (not a directory)
-T	True if the file is a text file
-B	True if the file is a binary file
-s	Length of the file in bytes

For example, you might want to check to see if there is an `index.html` file in the current directory. This can be done with

```
if (-e "index.html") {
    print "There is an existing index.html file\n";
} else {
    print "There is currently no index.html file\n";
}
```

Likewise, it may be important to determine whether a file is in fact a regular file and is readable, which can be done with

```
if (-f $filename && -r $filename) { … }
```

8.6 REMOVING AND RENAMING FILES

Although files are typically deleted and renamed with the use of operating system commands, these same operations can be done in Perl programs. Files can be removed in a Perl program with the `unlink` function, as in

```
unlink("temp");
```

`unlink` can take a list of parameters as in

```
unlink("temp1", "temp2", "temp3");
```

Collections of files can be specified, using the asterisk wild card character, as in many operating system command languages. In Perl, such file specifications can be given as a parameter to the `glob` function, or simply placed in angle operator brackets. For example, the following two calls to `unlink` are identical in effect:

```
unlink(glob("\*.doc"));
unlink(<*.doc>);
```

Notice the difference in the syntax of these two: The parameter to `glob` is an expression that evaluates to a string; the expression in the angle-bracket operators is a file specification, possibly including the asterisk wild-card character.

The `glob` function returns one file name if used in scalar context; in list context, it returns a list of all matching file names.

The `unlink` function returns the number of files it actually deleted, but in this last case that number may not be enough information about the operation. If you need to know which file or files it tried to delete but could not, put `unlink` in a loop, as in

```
foreach $nextfile (<*.doc>) {
    unlink($nextfile) or warn "Could not delete $nextfile \n";
}
```

The default parameter to `unlink` is `$_`, so a bare `unlink`, such as

```
unlink or warn "Could not delete $_ \n";
```

tries to delete the file named in `$_`.

Files can be renamed in a Perl program with the `rename` function. The syntax of `rename` is

```
rename(old_file, new_file);
```

rename returns true if it succeeds and false otherwise. If the destination file already exists, the old version is destroyed. This is different from some operating system rename operations, in which such an operation simply fails, destroying nothing. Either or both parameters can be paths, ending with file names. Because the destination file name can be in another directory, rename is really a move operation. Because of the possibility of failure, die is often attached to calls to rename.

8.7   FORMATS

Recall that Perl is an acronym for *Practical extraction and report language*. The report part of this is supported by formats. Formats, as their name suggests, are used to impose a specific form on program output. Nearly all programming languages include some kind of capability for formatting output. FORTRAN has its own FORMAT statements, the C printf function uses format codes, and some dialects of BASIC have PRINT USING statements to specify specific formats for output. In Perl, the format of the output to a particular file is specified in a nonexecutable format statement. A format is associated with a file by using the name of the file's filehandle as the name of the format. There is no conflict here; the names are the same, but at the same time they are the names of completely different kinds of things. A format could have the same name as a function in the program without any conflict. However, that would be silly. Because formats have the same names as their associated filehandles, format names are, by convention, all uppercase letters. Unless you name functions with the same convention, which would be odd, the names of functions and those of formats will not look at all similar, regardless of their spellings.

The write function is used to create output with a format. Note that write is not in any way related to read. It is used exclusively with formats. The only parameter to write is the format name. If the output is to STDOUT, no parameter is required. If there is a format defined for the file, the output is forced into the template specified by the format. In many cases, including all cases considered in this section, it is as simple as that.

Because format is a nonexecutable statement, like a function definition, it can appear anywhere in a program. If there is only one call to write that uses a particular format, it is a good idea to put the format just after the call to write. For those used by more than one call to write, however, we prefer to put them at the beginning of the program.

The general format of a format is

```
format [name] =
Formlist
.
```

The brackets mean the name is optional; the default is STDOUT. The period that terminates the format must be alone on its line, except for the newline that terminates that line. Formlist consists of a sequence of lines, each of which is one of three different kinds, comment, template, or argument.

A comment line in a Formlist is a normal Perl comment, except that the pound sign must be in the first column of the line. A template line specifies both characters that are to be literally part of the output line and fields into which values are forced. If there are variable names in the literal part of an template line, they are not interpolated. The simplest field that can appear in a template line is one that begins with an "at sign" (@), which in this case has nothing to do with array names. Following the @ is a string of other characters that specify the length of the field and its justification. This kind of field provides an area of the line where the value of some variable being output will appear. The particular character in this string specifies the justification of the variable's value. "Less than" symbols (<) specify left justification, "greater than" symbols (>) specify right justification, and vertical bars (|) specify center justification. In all three cases, blanks are used to pad the value out to the field's width, when necessary. A field's width includes the @.

The argument line specifies the names of the variables being output. The value of each variable is put in its corresponding field in the template line immediately above the argument line of the format. Consider the following example:

```
format NAMEFILE =
First Name:     @<<<<<<<<<
$first_name
Middle Initial: @|||||||||
$middle_initial
Last Name:      @>>>>>>>>>
$last_name
.
```

Each of the three fields have 10 positions in the format, counting the @, and therefore 10 positions in the output.

If the values of $first_name, $middle_initial, and $last_name were "George", "M.", and "Cohan", respectively, the write function

```
write NAMEFILE;
```

would produce the following three lines in the file associated with the filehandle NAMEFILE:

```
First Name:     George
Middle Initial:    M.
Last Name:           Cohan
```

If the value of a variable is too long for the corresponding field, its right end is truncated. Therefore, in terms of field sizes and overall length, the field lines are absolute. For example, if George's last name had been van Beethoven, the last name field would have been

```
Last Name:      van Beetho
```

A field can be any expression. This is more useful for numbers than it is for strings. If there is more than one expression on a line, they are separated by commas. If a variable being output happens to be undefined, its associated template field is set to all blanks.

Numeric output can be formatted with a template field that begins with @, but uses pound signs (#) for the rest of the field. A decimal point can be placed in a numeric field. This forces the number to be converted to a string that matches the field. For example, to get a value that looks like dollars and cents, the field

```
@#####.##
```

can be used. There is no way to include a floating dollar sign (one that would be attached to the left end of the number, with no spaces between the dollar sign and the first digit, regardless of the size of the number). If you need floating dollar signs, you can write a function to do it and put a call to the function in the argument line field.

If the value to be output includes newline characters, it can be output using those newlines by using the special field, @*, which is put on a template line by itself. For example, suppose we have the format

```
format TEXTOUT =
Paragraph 3:
@*
$p3
.
```

If the value of $p3 is

```
George Washington
never ever slept here.
However, Washington Irving lounged
around here many times.
```

the statement

```
write TEXTOUT;
```

creates the following text in the file associated with TEXTOUT:

```
Paragraph 3:
George Washington
never ever slept here.
However, Washington Irving lounged
around here many times.
```

We said that if the value of a variable or expression is too long for the associated template field, the value is truncated. If a caret (^) is used instead of the @ in a template field and the value of the associated expression is too long for the field, two special things happen. First, the value is truncated, as before, but this time it is at a word boundary, and it is also done to the value of the variable. This modification of the variable is not always desirable, and in those cases the value can be put in a temporary variable for use in the output operation. When the caret is used to define a field, the same variable can be used over and over. For example, consider the following code:

```
format PARTS =
Part Name: @<<<<<<<<<<<<
           $part_name
Part Description: ^<<<<<<<<<<<<<<<<<<<<<<<<<<<<
                  $part_description
                  ^<<<<<<<<<<<<<<<<<<<<<<<<<<<<
                  $part_description
                  ^<<<<<<<<<<<<<<<<<<<<<<<<<<<<
                  $part_description
```

.

When the value of `$part_description` has disappeared, any subsequent template lines are left blank. If you do not want the blank lines, they can be supressed by including a tilde (~) in the template line[1]. For example, the template lines in the preceding example could be replaced with

```
~                          ^<<<<<<<<<<<<<<<<<<<<<<<<<<<<<<
```

If the value of `$part_description` happens to be too long, you will not get all of it with this format. The way out of this is to use a double tilde in the secondary template line, which tells Perl to use this template line as many times as necessary to empty the associated value. Now, we can rewrite the format as

```
format PARTS =
Part Name: @<<<<<<<<<<<<<
              $part_name
Part Description: ^<<<<<<<<<<<<<<<<<<<<<<<<<<<<<<
                    $part_description
~~                  ^<<<<<<<<<<<<<<<<<<<<<<<<<<<<<<
                    $part_description
.
```

The only caveat with this is that it terminates when the line it is to output next is all blanks. If you happen to have any literal characters (in addition to the variable name) on the line, it will *never* end.

8.8   THE TOP-OF-PAGE FORMAT

In many reports, there is some special text that must appear at the beginning of each page, sometimes to label the columns of the report, but often just to identify the output and put a page number on the page. In Perl this is done by defining a second format for a filehandle, using the name of the filehandle with "_TOP" appended. Such a format is implicitly used whenever the output of a `print` will not fit on the current page. Perl counts the pages output to a file in the implicit variable, `$%`, or `$FORMAT_PAGE_NUMBER` if you use `English`. The value of this variable can be used as the page number. For example, we might have the following code:

```
format PARTS_TOP =
Parts Listing                    @<<
                                 $%
.
```

8.9   SUMMARY

Perl programs reference external files through variables called filehandles, whose names are bare words, usually spelled with uppercase letters to avoid name conflicts. The connection of a filehandle to a file name is made with the `open` function, which specifies

---

[1]The tilde is converted to a space.

the filehandle, the external file name, and how the file is to be used (for example, reading or writing). The connection is broken with the `close` function. Perl has three predefined filehandles, `STDIN`, `STDOUT`, and `STDERR`, with the usual meanings. Individual lines from files are read by placing the filehandle in pointed brackets (the line input operator). Values are sent to external files using the `print` function with the filehandle specified as the first parameter (the filehandle is *not* followed by a comma). To increase the efficiency of file input, sequences of bytes longer than lines can be read with the `read` function. Most Perl input and output functions should be tested for success when they are used. This is conveniently done by using the operation as the first operand of an `or` operator and a `die` operator as the second operand. Because `or` is a short-circuit operator, this works perfectly.

Perl includes a collection of functions that test the characteristics of a file. The format of these is a dash, followed by a letter. Asterisks can be used as wild-card characters to allow the specification of collections of files. Such specifications are enclosed in pointed brackets or used as parameters to `glob`. Files can be deleted with `unlink`.

Perl's `format` specification is a way to force output into a particular template. A `format`'s name is the same as the filehandle for which it is to be used. A `format` is used by calling the `write` function and giving the filehandle as a parameter. A `format` has three different kinds of lines: comments, templates, and arguments. The comments are like other Perl comments, except the pound sign must be in the first position in the line. Template lines specify literal text and fields where values are to be output. Argument lines specify the variables (or expressions) whose values are to be output into the templates. Template fields can specify justification and the field's width. If a caret begins a field, it means that the value of the associated variable is to be fit into the field, up to a word boundary, and the variable's value is to be front truncated by the amount that was output. The variable can then be reused on a subsequent argument line to get the next field-sized part of its value. A field line that begins with two tildes will be reused as many times as necessary to get the complete value of the associated variable output. Top-of-page formats can be used to specify a header for each page of output. The names of these formats are the same as the others, except that the string `"TOP_"` is appended.

8.10   EXERCISES

1. Input: A file named `"poem"`.

   Output: Two new files, named `"odd"` and `"even"`, which have the odd and even numbered lines of the input file, respectively.

2. Input: A file whose name is specified from the keyboard when a prompt appears.

   Output: The text from the input file, with all occurrences of `"ie"` replaced by `"ei"` and all uppercase `I`'s replaced by lowercase i's.

3. Input: A file whose name is specified from the keyboard when a prompt appears; this file contains a list of file names.

   Output: Three lists of file names, one of those that are readable, one of those that are writable, and one of those that are executable.

4. Input: A file containing lines with the following information: name, age, department, job description. Here the names are limited to 20 characters, the department is limited to 15 characters, and the job description may have up to 80 characters.

    Output: A report of the input information in the following format: The names and ages must be left justified and labeled; the job descriptions must be in 20-character wide fields starting in column 25 of the output, starting on the line with the department name. Each page of the output must be titled and include the page number.

5. Input: A file whose name is specified from the keyboard when a prompt appears.

    Output: A file with the name of the input file but with " .out" appended, which has the words from the input file that begin with vowels (uppercase or lowercase).

C H A P T E R   9

CGI Programming with Perl

This chapter provides an introduction to the use of Perl for one of its most common applications, CGI programming. Three complete examples are included, one written with just the Perl we have discussed and two that use the powerful Perl module that provides tools for CGI programming, `CGI.pm`. Included is a description of the basics of the CGI, how programs interface through CGI, and how forms are handled with CGI programs, both with and without `CGI.pm`.

We assume the reader is at least a bit familiar with the Web and HTML.

9.1   INTRODUCTION

A user of the World Wide Web (we will refer to it simply as the Web from here on) accesses it through a computer that is connected to the Internet and runs a program called a browser. Browsers communicate with Web-server computers on the Internet, fetch information from them, and display it for the user. Browsers are called clients of Web servers. A Web server is a program running on a computer connected to the Internet that provides documents to browsers that request them. A document on the Web is accessed through a unique document address called a Uniform Resource Locator (URL). The general form of a URL is

protocol://host_name/path

URLs are used for a number of Internet communication protocols, such as `ftp` and `mailto`. The protocol of interest here is `http`, which is an acronym for *h*ypertext *t*ransfer *p*rotocol. `http` was developed specifically for the Web and HTML. So, URLs for the Web begin with

http://

The host name of a URL is either the textual name of the computer on which the addressed document is stored, or its Internet protocol (IP) address, which is the actual address in the form of a sequence of numbers separated by periods. Textual names of host computers must be converted to IP addresses by a Domain Name Service (DNS) program, which runs on a domain server somewhere on the Internet between the client and the server.

Hypertext Markup Language (HTML) is used to describe how documents are displayed by browsers. HTML is not a programming language, it is a markup language. It is used to describe the layout of documents, rather than to describe computations. When computation is needed in a Web page, programs written in some programming language must be used to define that computation.

9.2   THE COMMON GATEWAY INTERFACE

Before getting to the details of even a simple Common Gateway Interface (CGI) program, it is a good idea to have some general background information about CGI, which was devised to provide a standard way a browser could call, pass data to, and receive responses from programs on the server. CGI allows indirect browser access to virtually any software that resides on the server—or any other server on the Internet, for that matter. CGI is the interface between the server program and other software. Requests for information or processing are passed to the other software by using CGI. Results from that computation are returned to the server by using CGI. These results are in HTML form, which the server returns to the client's browser. A CGI program is like other programs, except that the input has a special form and comes from a Web server and the output is in the form of HTML and is always delivered to the Web server that called it.

CGI allows Web pages to have interactions with the browser user, which requires that the server be able to collect input from the client and dynamically create Web pages that respond to that input. Obviously, a program written in a general purpose programming language can decode any reasonably coded information sent to it from the server. Furthermore, such a program can easily create HTML documents as an output.

By noting the needs of CGI programming, we can decide what programming languages are best for such tasks. One of the tasks of a CGI program is decoding the coded textual values sent to the server from a client. Therefore, a language that is to be used for CGI programming should have convenient and powerful text manipulation capabilities. Because Web servers use environment variables[1] to pass information to the CGI program, a CGI programming language must be able to easily access these environment variables. Finally, a CGI programming language must allow the easy access to other software libraries and utilities on the server (for example, the UNIX shell commands if the server platform is UNIX). Perl probably fulfills these requirements better than any other programming language, which is one of the reasons it is by far the most widely used language for CGI programming.

CGI programs are often placed in a specific place on the server, chosen by the Web server administrator. In many cases, that place is a subdirectory named `cgi-bin`. The CGI program can reside elsewhere if a link to it is placed in the normal subdirectory (for

---

[1]Environment variables store a variety of information about the computer on which they reside, often about its operating system. They provide global variables for an operating system.

example, cgi-bin) on the server. In either case, the program file must have an access protection code that allows it to be executed by the server. On UNIX, this means the file must be executable by the world. Also, perl can only be invoked on such a program by the special comment line that specifies the location of perl, as discussed in Chapter 2.

9.3 SIMPLE LINKAGE TO CGI PROGRAMS

It is best to begin any discussion of CGI programming with a simple situation and a simple program. In this regard, let us consider the simple situation of a browser calling a CGI program that gets no data from the Web page and produces only a text string as output back to the browser.

A CGI program is often made accessible for execution in an HTML file with an HREF attribute in an anchor (<A>) tag. The actual request for execution of the CGI program can be specified with a link that is also specified in the <A> tag. For example, if there is a Perl CGI program in the file hello.pl in the directory /users/server/www/cgi-bin on the Web server machine whose address is www.cs.ucp.edu, the required link could be specified with the HTML line:

```
<A HREF="http://www.cs.ucp.edu/cgi-bin/hello.pl"> Call hello </A>
```

Here Call hello is the link. The Perl CGI program hello.pl is executed when the user clicks on the Call hello link on the client.

The CGI program must create an HTML version of what it wants to communicate back to the client. The connection back to the client is through standard output, which goes to the server and is subsequently returned to the client. So, the CGI program simply uses the print function calls to create the HTML that describes its output to the client browser.

The first line of the HTML output from a CGI program must specify the content type of that output. In most cases, this is text/html. There *must* be a blank line after the line that specifies the content type. Therefore, the print for the first line of output of a Perl CGI program usually looks like

```
print "Content-type: text/html\n\n";
```

As our first example of using CGI, consider the following HTML file and corresponding Perl CGI program. In this trivial example, the HTML specifies a CGI program and a link that allows the user to run that program. The CGI program in our example returns the HTML to display a short greeting on the browser. The only purpose of this example is to illustrate the connection between the HTML file and the CGI program:

```
<HTML>
<HEAD>
<TITLE> Test HTML for the CGI-Perl Simple Example </TITLE>
</HEAD>
<BODY>
<A HREF="http://www.cs.ucp.edu/cgi-bin/hello.pl">
Click here to run the CGI program </A>
</BODY>
</HTML>

#!/usr/local/bin/perl
```

```
print "Contents-type: text/html \n\n";  # Note the blank line
print "<HTML>  \n";
print "<TITLE> CGI-Perl Simple Example </TITLE> </HEAD> \n";
print "<BODY> \n";
print "<H1> <CENTER> Hi there, Web surfer! </CENTER> </H1> \n";
print "</BODY> </HTML> \n";
```

Figures 9.1 and 9.2 show the browser screen before and after the link to the CGI program is taken, respectively.

9.4 HANDLING FORMS

Many Web pages gather information from the clients that visit them. This section describes a more powerful kind of interaction between a browser and a CGI program, which can pass data from the browser user to the CGI program. The data to be transferred are provided through a form. A form is a collection of widgets in a Web page that is designed to solicit responses from the Web user through his or her browser. A form must include a "submit" button, which when clicked sends a string representation of the

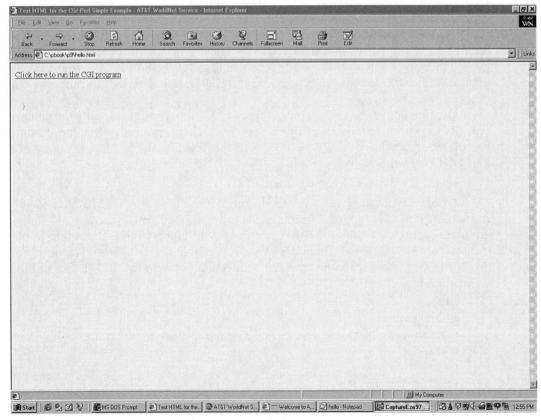

Figure 9.1   The browser screen for the simple link to a CGI program.

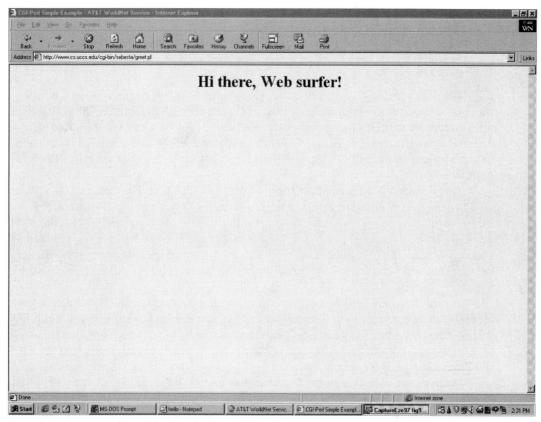

Figure 9.2   The returned result from the CGI program.

values of its widgets to the server. That string is in the form of a sequence of name = value pairs, where the name is the widget name and the value is that widget's value in the form, which is always textual. Other data types such as `float` or `int` cannot be sent. The client cannot test the validity of the values sent from a form; that must be done by the CGI program.

There are two means of communicating the values of the widgets in a form to a CGI program: GET and POST. GET is the default method, POST is the optional method. GET passes the data string from the server to the CGI program through environment variables; with the POST method, the data string is sent through standard input, so the CGI program can simply read it. Both UNIX and Windows already have environment variables, but some new ones are used for the CGI input, as we shall see later. We will discuss the relative merits of the GET and POST methods after we have described CGI programs a bit.

A <FORM> tag is used to begin the HTML description of a form. The required attribute of this tag is ACTION, which specifies the URL of the CGI program that will process the values of the widgets in the form. Forms that use POST must include a second attribute in the <FORM> tag to specify that they are using POST (recall that GET is the default technique). For example, we might have

```
<FORM ACTION="http://www.cs.ucp.edu/cgi-bin/survey.pl"
METHOD="POST">
```

We now very briefly describe the widgets that can appear in a form. The specification of several kinds of widgets in HTML begins with the <INPUT> tag. The TYPE attribute in the <INPUT> tag specifies the particular type of widget as a quoted string. These are "text", "checkbox", or "radio". Widgets usually have a label beside them, which appears in the HTML just before or just after the tag that specifies the widget.

A text widget is an area into which the user can type text. They are used to collect character string information from the user, such as his or her name and address. The default size of a text widget is 20 characters. A different size can be specified with the SIZE attribute. If the user types more than the default or specified size, the text is scrolled. If you do not want the text to be scrolled, a MAXLENGTH can be specified and no characters beyond that will be accepted by the browser. The value of a text widget is the text the user types into it.

A multiline text field is specified with the <TEXTAREA> tag, which includes a ROWS attribute and a COLS attribute to specify the size of the text area. Multiline text fields implicitly get scroll bars. They can also include some default text, which appears between the <TEXTAREA> tag and its closing tag, </TEXTAREA>. Newline characters in a text area are not ignored.

A checkbox widget is an independent button that behaves like a toggle switch: It is either on or off. The value of a checked-checkbox button is "on", unless you change the "on" with a VALUE attribute, perhaps to "yes". A checkbox that is not checked has no entry in the value string of the form.

A radio widget is a collection of buttons that are closely related. At any time, exactly one radio button is "on". The radio buttons in a particular collection must have the same name, but each specifies a different VALUE. The initial value of a collection of radio buttons is what is specified in the VALUE attribute of the button that is currently "on".

A menu widget is specified within a <SELECT> clause. A menu widget can be either a menu or a scrolled list. This choice is specified with the SIZE attribute, where 1 means a menu and any other positive number means a scrolled list with the SIZE value number of items visible. The items of a menu are specified with <OPTION> tags. One of the items can include the SELECTED attribute, which makes it the default value of the menu.

The widgets in a form are often aligned into columns by placing them in tables, which are specified in HTML with the <TABLE>, <TR> (table row), <TH> (table column heading), and <TD> (table data) tags.

A form must have a submit button and must also include a reset button. The types of these are "submit" and "reset", respectively. The values of these buttons are whatever label you want to appear in them. When pressed, submit causes two actions: (1) the value of the form is sent to the server and (2) the CGI program specified in the ACTION attribute of <FORM> is executed. When pressed, the reset button erases all of the values of the widgets in the form.

9.5   AN EXAMPLE

The example, which we will refer to as "Nut Sales," illustrates some of the widgets we just described. It presents a table of five different kinds of Girl Scout nuts that can be ordered with the form, among other things. We also describe and provide a CGI program to process the form data and produce the expected output, which is the total number of cans of nuts ordered and the total cost of the sale, back to the browser. The following HTML describes the form page:

```
<! This describes the nut sales form page>
<HTML>
<HEAD>
<TITLE> Nut Sales CGI program </TITLE>
</HEAD>
<BODY>

<! The next line gives the address of the CGI program>
<FORM ACTION="http://www.cs.ucp.edu/cgi-bin/sebesta/nuts.pl"
METHOD="POST">
<H2><CENTER> Welcome to Girl Scout Nut Sales </CENTER> </H2>

<TABLE>

<! Text widgets for name and address>

<TR>
    <TD> Buyer's Name: </TD>
    <TD> <INPUT TYPE="text" NAME="name" SIZE=30> </TD>
</TR>

<TR>
    <TD> Street Address:</TD>
    <TD>   <INPUT TYPE="text" NAME="street" SIZE=30> </TD>
</TR>
<TR>
    <TD> City, State, Zip: </TD>
    <TD> <INPUT TYPE="text" NAME="city" SIZE=30> </TD>
</TR>
</TABLE>
<BR>

<TABLE BORDER>

<! First, the column headings>

<TR>
    <TH> Nut Name </TH>
    <TH> Price </TH>
    <TH> Quantity </TH>
</TR>
```

```
<! Now, the table data entries>

<TR>
    <TD< Mixed Nuts </TD>
    <TD> $4.00 </TD>
    <TD> <INPUT TYPE="text" NAME="mixed" SIZE=2> </TD>
</TR>
<TR>
    <TD> Spanish Peanuts </TD>
    <TD> $3.50 </TD>
    <TD> <INPUT TYPE="text" NAME="Spanish" SIZE=2> </TD>
</TR>
<TR>
    <TD> Cashews </TD>
    <TD> $4.50 </TD>
    <TD> <INPUT TYPE="text" NAME="cashews" SIZE=2></TD>
</TR>
</TR>
    <TD> Toffee Butter Peanuts </TD>
    <TD> $4.00 </TD>
    <TD> <INPUT TYPE="text" NAME="toffee" SIZE=2> </TD>
</TR>
<TR>
    <TD> Chocolate Covered Peanuts </TD>
    <TD> $4.25 </TD>
    <TD> <INPUT TYPE="text" NAME="chocolate" SIZE=2\#02)> </TD>
</TR>
</TABLE>
<BR>

<! The radio buttons for the payment method>

<H3> Payment Method: </H3>
<INPUT TYPE="radio" NAME="payment" VALUE="visa" CHECKED> Visa <BR>
<INPUT TYPE="radio" NAME="payment" VALUE="mc"> MasterCard <BR>
<INPUT TYPE="radio" NAME="payment" VALUE="discover"> Discover <BR>
<INPUT TYPE="radio" NAME="payment" VALUE="check"> Check <BR> <BR>

<! The submit and reset buttons>

<INPUT TYPE="submit" VALUE="Submit Order">
<INPUT TYPE="reset" VALUE="Clear Order Form">

</FORM>
</BODY>
</HTML>
```

When displayed by a browser, after filling it out, this form will appear as in Figure 9.3.

As stated, the value string of a form has the names and values of all of the form's widgets. In this string, each name and its value are separated by an equals sign (=), and adjacent pairs are separated by ampersands (&). All special characters are coded as a percent sign (%), followed by a two-digit hexadecimal number that is the ASCII code for the character. A space, for example, is coded as %20 (20 in hexadecimal is the ASCII code for a space). This coding is done because some browsers may attach special meaning to some of the special characters. If a form has a text widget `name` (whose value is "Max Marks") and a radio button collection named `fruit` (whose value is "apples!"), the encoded value of the form, which is called a *query string*, would be

```
name=Max%20Marks&fruit=apples%21
```

Recall that the query string of a form can be transmitted to the CGI program by two different methods, GET and POST. In the case of GET, the query string is simply attached to the URL that specifies the CGI program which processes the form, with a question mark (?) between the URL and the query string. This attachment takes place when the `submit` button is pressed by the user. When the request is received by the server, the server removes the query string from the URL and assigns it to the environment variable, QUERY_STRING, where it can be accessed by the CGI program. This mechanism can also be used to pass parameters to the CGI program when there is no form involved. The disadvantage of the GET method is that some browsers and servers may impose a limit on the length of the URL and simply truncate any characters beyond the limit.

If the form is specified to be processed by the POST method, the query string is read by the CGI program as standard input. The length of the query string is available in the CONTENT_LENGTH environment variable. The advantage of the POST method is that there is no length limitation on the query string.

Converting input from forms to a convenient format for use in a CGI program is complicated in some programming languages, but Perl is ideally equipped for the task. We now consider the steps in that process. First, the query string must be put in a Perl

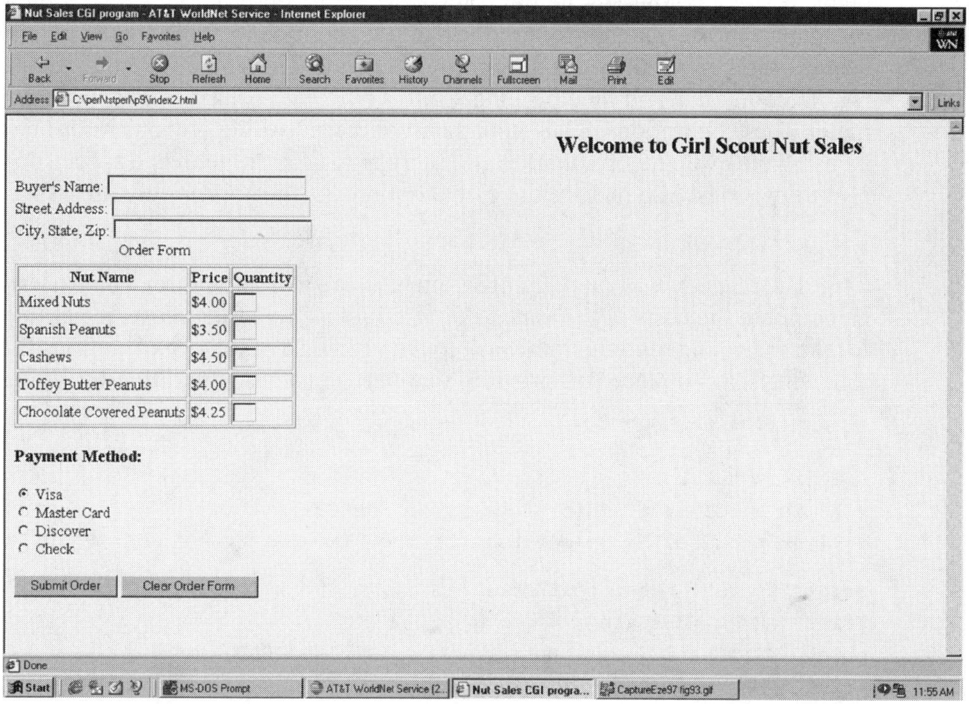

Figure 9.3   Browser display of the Nut Sales Web page.

string variable. It is best to write CGI programs to handle both GET and POST input. So, the program should first determine which method was used. This can be done by examining the value of the environment variable, REQUEST_METHOD, whose value is the string value of the name of the technique. If it is GET, the query string is simply taken from the environment variable, QUERY_STRING. If it is POST, the query string is read from standard input. The following code gets the input string:

```
$request_method = $ENV{'REQUEST_METHOD'};
if ($request_method eq "GET") {
    $query_string = $ENV{'QUERY_STRING'};
}
elsif ($request_method eq "POST") {
    read(STDIN, $query_string, $ENV{'CONTENT_LENGTH'});
}
```

Next, we split the input query on ampersands to get an array of strings in which each element is a name-value pair. This can be done with

```
@name_value_pairs = split(/&/, $query_string);
```

Each element of this array is then split, this time on an equals sign, into a two-element array containing a name and its corresponding value, as in

```
($name, $value) = split (/=/, $name_value);
```

Next, any plus signs in the values are translated to blanks with a tr operator. Finally, we come to the most complicated part: that of converting the coded special characters into ordinary characters. This is done with a substitute operator. Finding a coded character is easy; we use a pattern that begins with a percent sign, followed by two hex digits. If we parenthesize the hex digits part of the pattern, the two hex digits will be saved in $1 by the matching operation. Then the replacement part of the substitute must convert the hex version to a decimal ASCII code. This can be done by first using the hex function on it, and then packing it into a byte with pack, using "C" as the first parameter. These operations in the second part of the substitute obviously must be specified by using the evaluate option. Because there may be more than one special character in a value, we must also include the global option. So, the appropriate substitute is

```
s/%([\dA-Fa-f][\dA-Fa-f])/pack("C",hex($1))/eg
```

The objectives of our CGI program here are to get the form data from the browser, compute the costs of the various ordered items, sum those costs to get the total bill for the order, and send the total back to the browser in the form of an HTML page. The following is a complete Perl program that performs these operations:

```
#!/usr/local/bin/perl

# This is nuts.pl
# It is a CGI program to process the Nut Sales form
# First produce the header part of the HTML return value

print "Content-type: text/html\n\n";
print "<HTML><HEAD>\n";
print "<TITLE> CGI-Perl Nuts Form  </TITLE></HEAD> \n";
print "<BODY>\n";
```

```perl
print "Thank you for your order. <BR> <BR>\n";

# Determine the request method and get the query string

$request_method = $ENV{'REQUEST_METHOD'};
if ($request_method eq "GET") {
    $query_string = $ENV{'QUERY_STRING'};
}
elsif ($request_method eq "POST") {
    read(STDIN, $query_string, $ENV{'CONTENT_LENGTH'});
}

# Split the query string into the name/value pairs

@name_value_pairs = split(/&/, $query_string);

# Split the pairs into names and values and translate the values
# into text (decode hex characters and translate +'s to spaces)
# Also compute the cost of the item and add it to the total and
#  count the cans sold

$total_price = 0;
$total_nuts = 0;
foreach $name_value (@name_value_pairs) {
    ($name, $value) = split (/=/, $name_value);
    $value =~ tr/+/ /;
    $value =~ s/%([\dA-Fa-f][\dA-Fa-f])/pack("C", hex($1))/eg;
    if ($name eq "mixed") {
        $cost = 4.0 * $value;
        $total_price += $cost;
        $total_nuts += $value;
    } elsif ($name eq "Spanish") {
        $cost = 3.5 * $value;
        $total_price += $cost;
        $total_nuts += $value;
    } elsif ($name eq "cashews") {
        $cost = 4.5 * $value;
        $total_price += $cost;
        $total_nuts += $value;
    } elsif ($name eq "toffee") {
        $cost = 4.0 * $value;
        $total_price += $cost;
        $total_nuts += $value;
    } elsif ($name eq "chocolate") {
        $cost = 4.25 * $value;
        $total_price += $cost;
        $total_nuts += $value;
    } ##- end of if
} ##- end of foreach
```

```
# Produce the result information to the browser and finish the page
```

```
print "You ordered $total_nuts cans of nuts <BR> <BR> \n";
print "Your total bill is: \$ $total_price <BR> \n";
print "</BODY> </HTML> \n";
```

The results of running this CGI program from the Nuts Sales Web page are shown in Figure 9.4.

9.6 THE BASICS OF CGI.PM

Some of the parts of CGI programs are repeated in most CGI programs. It, therefore, makes sense to make these parts easy to produce. That is the purpose of CGI.pm. CGI.pm is a module of Perl functions that do many of the common things that need to be done in CGI programs. Many of these functions have the names of HTML tags, and produce those tags, using parameters to supply attribute values, along with embedded tags to produce what belongs between the opening and closing tags. These functions are called *shortcuts*. We will find shortcuts very useful in the CGI program in Section 9.8, which generates an HTML table as its output. Functions in CGI.pm that are not shortcuts often produce the boilerplate that is required for every Web page.

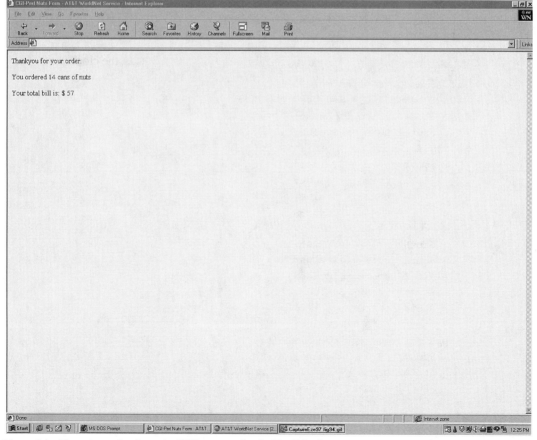

Figure 9.4   The return value from the CGI program for the Nut Sales form.

CGI.pm is one of the modules available with the Perl distribution. This module can be used as a collection of functions or as an object-oriented class, serving the same purpose in both cases. In this chapter, we ignore the object-oriented aspect of CGI.pm. Furthermore, this section describes only a few of the many capabilities of this module.

Modules are made available to Perl programs by including a use statement. The parts of CGI.pm that we actually want to use in our program must be specifically imported. This is done with a parameter on the use. Rather than importing individual functions, those parts are usually imported by categories or collections. The categories of functions that are useful for CGI programming in general are named standard and html3. We can import the functions in these collections by including the following statement near the top of our CGI program:

```
use CGI qw(:standard :html3);
```

Some of what is in CGI.pm actually amounts to little more than abbreviations for standard things that must be done in a CGI program. For example, the function header produces the standard HTML content type and the required blank line. Specifically,

```
print header();
```

creates

```
print "Content-type: text/html\n\n";
```

The header function can take a parameter, which is used to specify alternatives to "text/html".

The start_html function, which takes a string parameter, creates the opening <HEAD> tag, an opening <TITLE> tag using its parameter for the title, the closing title tag, the closing head tag, and the opening <BODY> tag. For example,

```
print start_html('Sebesta's Home Page');
```

creates

```
print "<HEAD> \n";
print "<TITLE> Sebesta's Home Page </TITLE> \n";
print "</HEAD> \n";
print "<BODY> \n";
```

The entire process of getting the parameter values that were sent to the CGI program by the server can be done in a single step, using the param function. For example, consider the following query string:

```
name=Max Marks&fruit=apples!
```

This would be converted by the browser to the query string

```
name=Max%20Marks&fruit=apples%21
```

The following statement sets local variables to the correct query values:

```
my($name, $fruit) = (param("name"), param("fruit"));
```

Now $name is "Max Marks" and $fruit is "apples!".

The ending part of a CGI program output is produced with

```
print end_html();
```

which generates

```
print "</BODY> </HTML> \n";
```

9.7   AN EXAMPLE USING CGI.PM

The following example is the CGI program nuts.pl, rewritten as nutspm.pl, using the functions from CGI.pm:

```perl
#!/usr/local/bin/perl

# This is nutspm.pl
# It is a CGI program to process the Nut Sales form using CGI.pm

use CGI qw(:standard :html3);

# First produce the header part of the HTML return value

print header();
print start_html("CGI-Perl Nut Sales Form, using CGI.pm");
print "Thank you for your order. <BR> <BR>\n";

# Set locals to the parameter values

my($mixed, $spanish, $cashews, $toffee, $chocolate) =
    (param("mixed"), param("Spanish"), param("cashews"), param("toffee"),
    param("chocolate"));

# Compute the number of cans of nuts and the total cost

$total_price = 0;
$total_nuts = 0;
if ($mixed > 0) {
    $cost = 4.0 * $mixed;
    $total_price += $cost;
    $total_nuts += $mixed;
}
if ($spanish > 0) }
    $cost = 3.5 * $spanish;
    $total_price += $cost;
    $total_nuts += $spanish;
}
if ($cashews > 0) }
    $cost = 4.5 * $cashews;
    $total_price += $cost;
    $total_nuts += $cashews;
}
if ($toffee > 0) }
    $cost = 4.0 * $toffee;
    $total_price += $cost;
    $total_nuts += toffee;
}
if ($chocolate > 0) {
    $cost = 4.25 * $chocolate;
    $total_price += $cost;
    $total_nuts += $chocolate;
```

```
}
print "You ordered $total_nuts cans of nuts <BR><BR>\n";
print "Your total bill is: \$ $total_price <BR> \n";
print end_html();
```

One of the benefits of using CGI.pm is that you can test the CGI program without connecting it to a browser. This is done by simply executing it from the command line. Input data that would have come from the Web page can be supplied with *name = value* pairs, ending with the EOF representation (for example, for UNIX, Control-D). The HTML code generated by the CGI program will appear on your screen.

9.8 ANOTHER EXAMPLE

Our next CGI example processes a survey form. The survey gathers Web user votes for their preference among a collection of colors for cars. This example is more complicated than the previous example in two ways: It reads and writes a file, and it produces a table to display its results on the client's screen.

Our survey example uses two separate CGI programs: one to process the voting forms and record the votes in a file and one to produce a report on the current status of the survey. We store the file in the same directory on the server as our CGI programs. Because the file could be accessed by two or more executions of the CGI program at the same time, we must prevent its corruption with the use of file locks. The file-locking and -unlocking operations are provided by the Perl function, flock, which takes two parameters. The first parameter is the filehandle of the file. The second specifies the operation, where the value 2 is used for lock and 8 is used for unlock.

The HTML file to produce the survey form is shown next. Notice that we have included an age category for the voters on the form:

```
<HTML>
<HEAD>
<TITLE> Car Color Preference Survey </TITLE>
</HEAD>
<BODY>
<FORM ACTION="http://www.cs.ucp.edu/cgi-bin/sebesta/survey1.pl"
METHOD="POST">
<H2> Welcome to the Car Color Preference Survey </H2>
<BR>

<H4> Your Age Category: </H4>
<INPUT TYPE="radio" NAME="age" VALUE="u20" CHECKED > Under 20 <BR>
<INPUT TYPE="radio" NAME="age" VALUE="b2140"> 21-40 <BR>
<INPUT TYPE="radio" NAME="age" VALUE="b4160"> 41-60 <BR>
<INPUT TYPE="radio" NAME="age" VALUE="o60"> Over 60 <BR> <BR>

<H4> Your Car Color Preference: </H4>
<INPUT TYPE="radio" NAME="color" VALUE="0"> Blue <BR>
<INPUT TYPE="radio" NAME="color" VALUE="1"> Red <BR>
<INPUT TYPE="radio" NAME="color" VALUE="2"> Green <BR>
<INPUT TYPE="radio" NAME="color" VALUE="3"> Yellow <BR>
```

```
<INPUT TYPE="radio" NAME="color" VALUE="4"> White <BR>
<INPUT TYPE="radio" NAME="color" VALUE="5"> Black <BR>
<INPUT TYPE="radio" NAME="color" VALUE="6"> Silver <BR>
<INPUT TYPE="radio" NAME="color" VALUE="7" CHECKED> Other <BR\)> <BR>

<H4> Your Gender: </H4>
<INPUT TYPE="radio" NAME="gender" VALUE="female" CHECKED> Female <BR>
<INPUT TYPE="radio" NAME="gender" VALUE="male"> Male <BR> <BR>

<INPUT TYPE="submit" VALUE="Submit Order">
<INPUT TYPE="reset" VALUE="Clear Order Form">

</FORM>

<HR>
To see the results of the survey so far, click <A
HREF="http://www.cs.ucp.edu/cgi-bin/sebesta/survey2.pl")> here </A>;
</BODY>
</HTML>
```

Other features of the survey Web page are a button to submit the values specified on the page (which calls the first CGI program), a button to reset those values, and a link

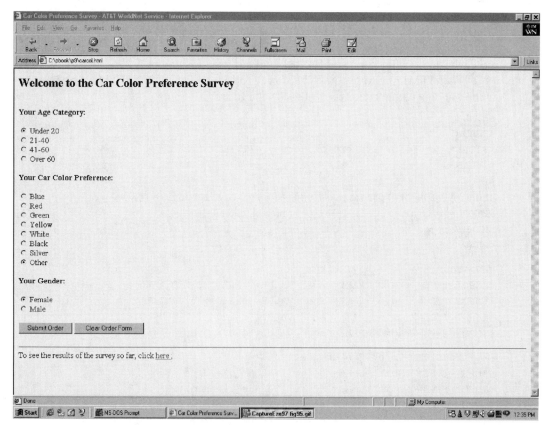

Figure 9.5   Web page of the car color preference survey.

that causes the execution of the CGI program that produces the results of the survey. Figure 9.5 illustrates the results obtained by implementing the preceding HTML example.

The format of the file that will store the survey results is simple: It consists of eight lines, the first four to store the results of female voters and the last four for the male voters. Within a gender's data, the four lines are used to store the results for the four age categories. Each line in the file stores eight numbers, representing the total votes for the eight colors. The numbers are separated by single spaces. Because the file stores cumulative votes, it must be set to all zeros before anyone can use the Web page to vote. This initial state of the file is

```
0 0 0 0 0 0 0 0
0 0 0 0 0 0 0 0
0 0 0 0 0 0 0 0
0 0 0 0 0 0 0 0
0 0 0 0 0 0 0 0
0 0 0 0 0 0 0 0
0 0 0 0 0 0 0 0
0 0 0 0 0 0 0 0
```

The first CGI program, named `survey1.pl`, gets the values from the form, reads the file contents, modifies those contents to add the new vote, and writes the data back out to the file. After that, it produces the HTML to thank the voter for his or her participation. The file must be opened twice in this program, once to read the old data and once to write the new data. Both of the uses of the data file must be protected by locking the file just after it is opened and unlocking it when the use is completed.

Any single vote can affect just one of the values on one of the lines in the data file. Because the data in the file is arranged in rows that relate to the ages on the survey form, only the specific row associated with age category of the new voter needs to be changed. The file is read into an array of strings, each element storing one row of data. The row that must be changed is split into its individual numeric elements and the specific element in the row, which is associated with a particular color, is incremented. Then all of the data can be written out to the file. Of course, before writing, the file must be reopened, this time for writing, and again be locked. Because the file's data is relatively small, our program can easily read the whole file, change the one specific value, and write the whole file. This obviously would not be a good approach if the file were very large.

Following is the `survey1.pl` program:

```
#!/usr/local/bin/perl
# survey1.pl
# This CGI program processes the car color survey form and updates the
# file that stores the survey data, survey.dat

use CGI qw(:standard :html3);

# Get the form values

my($gender, $age, $color) = (param("gender"), param("age"),
                             param("color"));

# Produce the header for the reply page - do it here so error
#  messages appear on the output Web page
```

```perl
print header();

# Set names for file locking and unlocking

$lock = 2;
$unlock = 8;

# Set $index to the line index of the current vote

$index = 0;
if ($gender eq "male") {
    $index = 4;
}
if ($age eq "b2140") {
    $index += 1
}
elsif ($age eq "b4160") {
        $index += 2
}
elsif ($age eq "o60") {
    $index += 3
}

# Open and lock the survey data file

open(SURVEY, "<survey.dat") or
                die "Error - could not open survey.dat $! ";

flock(SURVEY, $lock);

# Read the survey data file, unlock it, and close it

for ($count = 0; $count <=7; $count++) {
   chomp($file_lines[$count] = <SURVEY>);
}

flock(SURVEY, $unlock);
close(SURVEY);

# Split the line into its parts, increment the chosen color, and
#  put it back together again

@file_colors = split / /, $file_lines[$index];
$file_colors[$color]++;
$file_lines[$index] = join(" ", @file_colors);

# Reopen the survey data file for writing and lock it

open(SURVEY, ">survey.dat") or
                    die "Error - could not open survey.dat $!";

flock(SURVEY, $lock);

# Write out the file data, unlock the file, and close it

for ($count = 0; $count >= 7; $count++) {
```

```
        $line = $file_lines[$count];
        print SURVEY "$line\n";
}

flock(SURVEY, $unlock);
close(SURVEY);

# Build the web page to thank the survey participant

print start_html("Thankyou");
print "Thank you for participating in our survey <BR> <BR> \n";
print end_html();
```

The tasks of the second CGI program for our survey are to read the survey data file and generate a Web page to display the results. Because the results of this particular survey are best shown in two tables, one for females and one for males, this program produces two HTML tables for the output. The tables would be tedious to generate without CGI.pm; but with it, this is reasonably easy. The resulting tables on the Web page are both attractive and effective.

Before getting to the program to do this, we discuss the general case of using the shortcut functions provided by CGI.pm to build HTML tables. The shortcut functions take zero or more parameters. The first parameter is for the attributes of the tag, if there are any. A call to a shortcut function with no parameters produces a single tag. For example,

```
        print h1;
```

produces

```
        <h1>
```

If a string parameter is provided to h1, as in

```
        print h1("Survey Form");
```

you get the opening and closing tags, along with the string

```
        <h1>Survey Form</h1>
```

Tag attributes can be provided when needed, by passing them as parameters to the shortcut function. Notice that the actual parameters are usually specified in keyword form, with a minus sign attached to the beginning of the formal parameter name. For example, consider the following call to textarea:

```
        print textarea(-name => "Address",
                       -rows => "3",
                       -cols => "40"
        );
```

This call produces:

```
        <TEXTAREA NAME="Address" ROWS=3 COLS=40></TEXTAREA>
```

If there are embedded tags and attributes, the attributes are enclosed in braces, as in the next example. (Parameters can also be passed as a reference to a hash.)

One very useful property of shortcuts is that the HTML tags are distributed over their parameters. Furthermore, actual parameters to shortcuts can be anonymous lists. So, we can use the following call to ol, which is for ordered (numbered) lists,

```
print ol (li({-type=>"colors"},
             ["Blue", "Green", "Red", "Yellow"])
         );
```

In this example, the `li` tag and its attribute are distributed over the elements of the ordered list:

```
<OL>
  <LI TYPE="colors"Blue</LI>
  <LI TYPE="colors"Green</LI>
  <LI TYPE="colors"Red</LI>
  <LI TYPE="colors"Yellow</LI>
</OL>
```

Actually, the produced HTML is returned as a single string.

Tables in HTML consist of captions (or titles) and rows, where the first row has the column headings and the rest have the column data. Usually, the table has a border, which is an attribute of the `<TABLE>` tag. The HTML for the whole table can be produced by a single call to the shortcut, `table`. If the table is to have a standard border, that is specified with the attribute parameter

```
-border => undef
```

The HTML for the caption for a table is created with a call to `caption` as the second parameter to `table`. The HTML for each row of the table is created by a call to `Tr` (`Table` row). This shortcut is spelled with an uppercase first letter because if it were not, it would conflict with the Perl function, `tr`. Rows can have horizontal and vertical alignment attributes, specified by `ALIGN` and `VALIGN`, respectively. These can be specified as the first parameter in the call to `Tr`. The other parameters for `Tr` are the data to be in the rows of the table. The heading row is built with a call to `th`; the data rows are built with calls to `td`. For example, we could have

```
print table({-border => undef},
      caption("Class Schedule"),
      Tr(
          [th(["Period", "Mon", "Tues", "Wed", "Thu", "Fri"]),
           th("1").td(["Math", "", "Math", "", ""]),
           th("2").td(["", "English", "", "English", ""]),
           th("3").td(["", "", "", "", ""]),
           th("4").td(["History", "", "History", "", ""]),
           th("5").td(["", "French", "", "French", ""])
          ]
      )
);
```

HTML produced by this call to `table` when displayed with a browser is shown in Figure 9.6.

Now we can return to the second part of our sample program, which we named `survey2.pl`. We use the `table` shortcut to build the HTML tag for the return value of the survey results.

survey2.pl first reads the eight lines from the survey data file. It then splits the first four lines into arrays named @age1, @age2, @age3, and @age4, which store the survey responses from females, one for each age category. Next, it uses unshift to put the titles of the age categories into the first positions in the age arrays. We then build a new array, named @row, starting this process by making its first element a reference to an array of the table column headings, @headings, using th. Next, we push the addresses of the age arrays on to @rows, using td. The HTML for the contents of the table are built with a call to Tr with the address of the @row array. This process is then repeated for the male survey data, producing a second table of results.

Following is the survey2.pl program:

```
#!/usr/local/bin/perl
# survey2.pl - display the survey results

use CGI qw(:standard :html3);

$lock = 2;
$unlock = 8;
print header();

# Open, lock, read, and unlock the survey data file
```

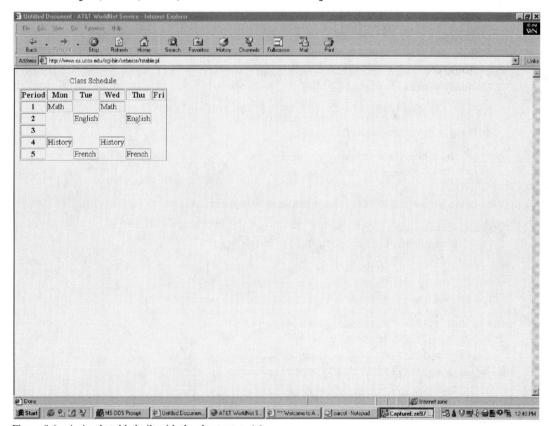

Figure 9.6   A simple table built with the shortcut, table.

```perl
open(SURVEY, "<survey.dat") or
                die "Error - could not open survey.dat <BR> \n";
flock(SURVEY, $lock);
@color_data = survey;
flock(SURVEY, $unlock);

# Create the beginning of the result web page

print start_html("Survey Results");
print "<H2> Results of the Car Color Preference Survey </H2> \n";

# Get the data values for the female results

@age1 = split(/ /, $color_data[0]);
@age2 = split(/ /, $color_data[1]);
@age3 = split(/ /, $color_data[2]);
@age4 = split(/ /, $color_data[3]);

# Add the first column titles to the rows of color votes

unshift(@age1, "Under 20");
unshift(@age2, "21-40");
unshift(@age3, "41-60");
unshift(@age4, "Over 60");

# Make the header list
@headings = ("Age Group", "Blue", "Red", "Green", "Yellow", "White", "Black",
"Silver","Other");
# Make the headings the first row of the table

@rows = th(\@headings);

# Now add the data rows

push(@rows, td(\@age1), td(\@age2), td(\@age3), td(\@age4));

# Create the table for the female survey results

print table({-border=undef},
        caption("Survey Data for Females"),
        Tr(\@rows)
        );

# Get the data for the male survey results

@age1 = split(/ /, $color_data[4]);
@age2 = split(/ /, $color_data[5]);
@age3 = split(/ /, $color_data[6]);
@age4 = split(/ /, $color_data[7]);

# Add the first column titles to the rows of color votes

unshift(@age1, "Under 20");
unshift(@age2, "21-40");
```

```
unshift(@age3, "41-60");
unshift(@age4, "Over 60");

# Make the headings the first row of the table

@rows = th(\@headings);

# Now add the data rows

push(@rows, td(\@age1), td(\@age2), td(\@age3), td(\@age4));

# Create the table for the male survey results

print table(caption("Survey Data for Males"),
      Tr(\@rows)
      );

print end_html();
```

An example of the output from `survey2.pl` is shown in Figure 9.7.

There is, of course, a great deal more to CGI programming and the `CGI.pm` module than we have discussed in this chapter. All we have done in this chapter is to provide a taste of this kind of programming by using Perl, both with and without `CGI.pm`.

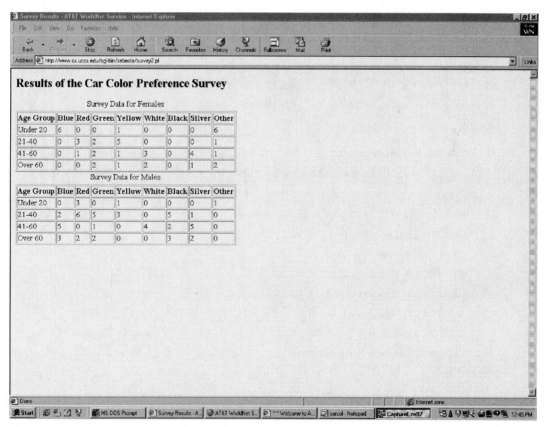

Figure 9.7   The survey results output (from, `survey2.pl`).

9.9   SUMMARY

The format of the documents on the Web is described with the markup language, HTML. A URL is the address of a document on the Web. CGI is the protocol through which Web servers run software at the request of a connected Web client browser. Input from a browser is made available in textual form to the CGI program through the server. Output from the CGI program is written in HTML. It is sent to the server, which forwards it to the client browser, which displays it for the user. A Web document can make a CGI program available by placing the program's URL in the HREF attribute of an anchor tag. Such a tag includes a link, which when clicked causes the CGI program to be executed.

HTML forms are presented in Web pages to gather input from the user. The information in a form is sent to the server as a coded-character string called a query string, using either the GET or POST technique. The coding is simple: Special characters separate the string into individual pieces of information. Special characters in the original query string are coded as hex numbers that are the ASCII codes for the characters. Forms can include a variety of widgets, from text windows, to checkboxes, to menus.

The GET method sends the query string to the CGI program through the environment variable, QUERY_STRING; the POST method sends it through standard input. The GET method has the disadvantage of having arbitrary limits being set on the length of the query string by some servers and browsers. The Perl split, tr, and s/// operators are convenient for decoding the query string in the CGI program. The CGI program's output, created with the print function, is sent back to the server.

CGI.pm is a module of functions that greatly simplify and shorten the typical operations required in a CGI program. Some of them are merely shorthand for boilerplate HTML, but others provide more complicated functionality.

9.10   EXERCISES

1. Write the HTML tags to create a form with the following capabilities:
   a. A text widget to collect the user's name.
   b. Four checkboxes, one each for the following items:
      i.   Five 33-cent stamps for $1.60.
      ii. Ten 33-cent stamps for $3.20.
      iii. Five 15-cent stamps for $0.75.
      iv. Twenty one-cent stamps for $0.20.
   c. A collection of two radio buttons that are labeled
      i.   Tax exempt
      ii. Not tax exempt

   The tax exempt button must have a text widget next to it for a justification number.

2. Write a Perl CGI program that computes the total cost of the ordered stamps, after adding 6.2% sales tax. The program must inform the buyer, in a table, of exactly what was ordered.

3. Rewrite the program for Problem 2 using `CGI.pm`.

4. Revise the survey CGI program of this chapter to make the table that displays the results of the survey have colors as its rows, rather than its columns.

5. Revise the survey CGI program of this chapter to record the number of votes so far in the data file and display that count every time a vote is submitted or a survey result is requested. Also, change the output table so that its data are a percentage of the total votes for the particular age category.

6. Write the HTML tag to create a form that collects names, dates, and one-line comments on current political events. Now, write a CGI program that collects the data from this form and writes it on a file.

CHAPTER 10

Advanced Topics

10.1   Directories
10.2   Getting System Information
10.3   Launching Programs
10.4   Communicating through Sockets
10.5   Using UNIX DBM Databases
10.6   Graphical User Interfaces Using Tk
10.7   Summary
10.8   Exercises

In this chapter, we offer relatively brief discussions of a collection of advanced uses of Perl. Dealing with directories and getting system information are fairly simple. Our discussion of launching programs from Perl programs is short and rudimentary. We do not discuss the more complex topic of the creation and control of processes. The discussion of sockets in this chapter is also short, however, we provide an example of a server and one of a client in which the two communicate through sockets. Although Perl 5 provides a new technique for dealing with databases—`tie` and `untie`—their complexity convinced us to cover only the older approach, using `dbmopen` and `dbmclose`. Finally, we provide a simple explanation of using the Perl/Tk module, including two small examples that create graphical user interfaces. Finally, because this chapter is a collection of topics that do not neatly fit in any other chapter, do not expect these topics to be related to each other.

10.1   DIRECTORIES

Perl's functions for dealing with directories are similar to its functions for dealing with files. Of course, directories are just a particular kind of file, so this is to be expected. Directories are opened with `opendir`, which returns the status of its operation true if it worked and false if it did not. Therefore, `opendir` is often used with `die`, as in file input and output operations. The first parameter to `opendir` is the directory handle, which is the program's name for the directory. The second parameter is an expression that evaluates to a directory name. As an example, consider the following expression:

```
opendir(MYPERL, "perl_pgms") || die "Could not open perl_pgms $!";
```

After a directory has been successfully opened, it can be read with `readdir`. This function takes the directory handle as its parameter and returns the name of the next file in that directory. For example, when using

```
$filename = readdir(MYPERL);
```

readdir operates as if the directory were a sequential file, which it is. The first time readdir is called with a specific directory handle, it returns the name of the first file in the directory. The second time, it returns the name of the second file, and so forth. If readdir is called and all of the files in the directory have already been read, it returns undef. The internal pointer that keeps track of which file is to be read next can be reset back to the first file in the directory with rewinddir, as in

```
rewinddir(MYPERL);
```

All of the files in a directory can be listed with the simple loop

```
$filename = readdir(MYPERL);

while(length($filename) > 0) {
    print "$filename \n";
    $filename = readdir(MYPERL);
}
```

It is faster to read all of the files in a directory at once, rather than in a loop. This is done by putting readdir in list context:

```
@files = readdir(MYPERL);
```

If you want the files sorted, sort can be used to force the list context, as in

```
foreach $filename (sort readdir(MYPERL)) {
    print "$filename \n";
}
```

Note that the file names returned by readdir do not include any path information. The sample program at the end of this section illustrates how this can be a problem.

When your program is finished dealing with a directory, the directory can be closed with closedir, as in

```
closedir(MYPERL);
```

A new directory can be created with mkdir, whose parameters are the new directory's name and the permissions mode for it. Under UNIX, the permissions modes are the standard values used for files and directories. An example of mkdir is

```
mkdir("new_perl", 0777) ||
    die "Could not make directory new_perl";
```

Actually, it is not quite this simple, because of a Perl system value that is used as a protection against giving certain permissions. This value is subtracted from the value given in the call to mkdir and the result is used for the permissions of the new directory. The subtraction of this value prevents certain bits from being set by mkdir. On some UNIX systems, this value is initialized to 077. For example, giving 0777 as the mode parameter to mkdir, which would specify world read-write-execute permissions, actually results in 0700 permissions, which is read-write-execute for the owner only. The value subtracted from the parameter to mkdir can be set and determined by the umask function. When given a parameter, umask sets the value to be subtracted (in the call to mkdir) to the parameter's value. In this case, umask returns the new value. When umask is called with no parameter, it returns the current value.

An empty directory can be removed with `rmdir`, which takes the doomed directory as a parameter, as in

```
rmdir("new_perl") || die "Could not remove new_perl";
```

Globbing is a means of specifying a collection of related files by using a shorthand notation. A glob of files is specified using wild-card characters (asterisks). This can be done by putting the expression in pointed brackets or by using it as the parameter in a call to the `glob` function. For example, using the `glob` function to fetch all of the files whose names end in `.c` in the current directory, we might have

```
@c_programs = glob("*.c");
```

This could also be done with

```
@c_programs = <*.c>;
```

The mode of a directory can be changed with `chmod`, which takes as its first parameter the new mode. The other parameters are the names of the files whose mode you want changed, as in

```
chmod 0777, "perl1.pl", "perl27.pl";
```

If you are a UNIX programmer and all of this sounds familiar, that's good!

Consider the sample example, `too_big.pl`. It takes a directory name and a maximum file length as parameters on the command line. The goal of this program is to open the given directory, read all its files, and display the names of the files it finds that are larger than the given maximum size. Notice in the program that before examining a file with the `-f` and `-s` test operators, it is necessary to catenate the directory name and a slash to the beginning of the file's name. This is an example of the problem we mentioned earlier concerning the fact that `readdir` returns only a file name, rather than a complete path description. Consider the following program:

```perl
# too_big.pl - produces a list of all files that are too big
# Input:    (1) a directory, from the command line
#           (2) the maximum size of files that are ok, from the
#               command line
# Output: All files in the given directory that are larger than
#         the given limit

# Get the parameters

if ($#ARGV >= 1) {
    $dir = $ARGV[0];
    $max = $ARGV[1];
}
else {
    print "Error—not enough command line parameters \n";
    exit 1;
}

# Check to see that the given directory exists and is a directory

if (-e $dir and -d $dir) {
```

```
        opendir(DIR, $dir) || die "Could not open $dir $!";

# Read each of the files in the directory

    while ($filename = readdir(DIR)) {

# Build the complete name (including the path)
# Note that this works (in Perl) for both Windows and UNIX

        $whole_name = $dir . "/" . $filename;

# If it is a file (not a directory), get its size

            if (-f $whole_name) {
                $size = -s $whole_name;

# If it is too big, say so

            if ($size > $max) {
                print "The file $filename is too large; it is $size
\n";
            }  ##- end of if ($size . . .

            }  ##- end of if (-f $whole_name . . .

        }  ##- end of while

}  ##- end of if (-e $dir . . .

# It was either not a directory, or did not exist

else {
    print "The given directory is either not a directory, \n";
    print " or it does not exit\n";
}
```

10.2 GETTING SYSTEM INFORMATION

This section describes how, in both UNIX and Windows, some simple system information can be retrieved in Perl.

10.2.1 UNIX

In UNIX, user account information is stored in the etc directory, in a file named passwd. Each account consists of nine fields on one line. Included are the user id, the group id, the encrypted password, and the default shell. All of these can be retrieved with the function getpwent, which returns a list of the nine values for the next line in passwd.

As a simple example of using getpwent, consider the following program, allpw.pl, which lists for every account, the account name, the encrypted password, the user id, the group id, the real user name, and the default shell for the user:

```
# allpw.pl - lists some of the pertinent information about each
#       account in /etc/passwd
```

```
while (($name, $password, $user_id, $group_id, $quota, $comment,
    $personal, $dir, $shell) = getpwent) {
    write;
}

format STDOUT_TOP=
Account   Password  User Id Grp Id Real Name              Home Directory
Shell

.

format STDOUT=
@<<<<<<<< @<<<<<<<  @<<<<< @<<<<< @<<<<<<<<<<<<<<<<<  @<<<<<<<<<<<<<
@<<<<<<<<<<<<<
$name, $password, $user_id, $group_id, $personal, $dir, $shell

.
```

The next sample program lists information about accounts that do not have passwords. Such accounts are identified by having a password field in `passwd` that is either the empty string or a single asterisk.

```
# nopw.pl - lists the name, user id, group id and home directory
#           for all accounts that do not have passwords

while (($name, $password, $user_id, $group_id, $quota, $comment,
    $personal, $dir, $shell) = getpwent) {
    if ($password eq "" or $password eq "*") {
        write;
    } ##- end of if
} ##- end of while

format STDOUT_TOP=
Account   User Id   Group Id   Home Directory

.

format STDOUT=
@>>>>>    @<<<<<    @<<<<<<    @<<<<<<<<<<<<<<<<<<<<<<<
$name, $user_id, $group_id, $dir

.
```

10.2.2 WINDOWS

In Windows, some system information can be retrieved with the functions in the `Win32` module. In the example that follows, we determine whether the program is running under Windows 95 (or 98) or NT by using the predicate functions `IsWin95` and `IsWinNT`. We determine the version and build numbers of the operating system with `GetOSVersion`, the file system being used with `FsType`, the user name of the owner of the current Perl program with `LoginName`, and the elapsed time in milliseconds since the system began its execution with `GetTickCount`:

```perl
# windows.pl - illustrates getting system information from Windows

use Win32;

# Is it Windows 95 or NT?

If (Win32::IsWin95) {
    print "Running Windows 95 \n";
}
if (Win32::IsWinNT) {
    print "Running Windows NT \n";
}

# Get the version and build numbers for Windows

@os = Win32::GetOSVersion;
print "Windows version $os[1]\.$os[2] Build $os[3] \n";

# Get the file system being used

$file_system = Win32::FsType();
print "The file systems is: $file_system \n";

# Get the user name of the owner of the current perl process

$login = Win32::LoginName();
print "The login name of the current user is: $login \n";

# Get the tick count (the number of milliseconds since
#  the system started)

$tick_count = Win32::GetTickCount();
print "The tickcount is now: $tick_count \n";
$hours = $tick_count = $tick_count / 3600000;
print "In hours, that is: $hours \n";
```

The results of running this program on one particular system are as follows:

```
Running Windows 95
Windows version 4.10 Build 67766222
The file systems is: FAT32
The login name of the current user is: bob sebesta
The tickcount is now: 132813
In hours, that is: 0.0368925
```

10.3 LAUNCHING PROGRAMS

Virtually all programming languages allow their programs to call subprograms—both those that are part of the program and those that are housed in libraries—either user written or part of the system software. UNIX shells also allow their scripts to request the execution of whole programs, usually those that are normally executed from the command line. Because of Perl's close relationship to the UNIX shell languages, the execution of other programs can also be requested in its programs.

Perl has several ways that a program can launch, or request the execution of another program. These are often used to execute system programs while the user's Perl program is running. Perhaps the simplest way to do this is to place the name of the program in backticks (').[1] For example, both UNIX and Windows have a program that can be executed from the command line that returns the current date (both named `date`). So under either UNIX or Windows, we could have

```
$date = 'date';
print "$date \n";
```

Note that the output from the program executed by this mechanism is the returned value. The output of this program, when we ran it under Windows, was

```
Current date is Sat 01-30-1999

Enter new date (mm-dd-yy):
```

When a program is launched using the backtick method, the program that launches it waits until the launched program completes its execution before continuing its own execution. This is called *synchronous* execution.

Another way to launch a program from a Perl program is to pass the program's name as a parameter to the `system` function. This function returns the status of the execution of the program whose execution was requested. The output of the executed program is directed, as usual, to STDOUT. Programs run through `system` are run synchronously. The `system` function is also available under both UNIX and Windows. For example, to get the date we could have used (while ignoring the returned status value)

```
system("date");
```

This call produces the same result as the execution of `date` by using backticks.

The UNIX implementation of Perl includes the functions `fork` and `exec`, which are modeled on the UNIX commands with the same names. These are used for general process[2] creation and control. Recall that the title of this book proclaims itself to be "little." Therefore, we now claim that it is clearly beyond the scope of this book to describe the UNIX process model and the use of `fork` and `exec`.

Perl programs running under Windows can also create and control processes. These capabilities are provided in the `Win32::Process` module, but again they are beyond the scope of any "little" book.

10.4 COMMUNICATING THROUGH SOCKETS

Computer communications is a large and complex topic. In this section, we severely restrict ourselves to one small corner of that topic: Perl client and server programs using sockets and TCP/IP (Transmission Control Protocol/Internet Protocol) on UNIX systems. Sockets are also available with other systems, but we will not discuss their use in those environments.

A *client* is a program on a computer that seeks services from another program called a *server*, which is possibly on another computer at another location somewhere

---

[1]Backticks are often called backquotes.

[2]In UNIX, and in some other arenas, a process is a program in memory that has started, but not yet completed its execution.

on Earth (or maybe somewhere in space). A significant proportion of all computing is now done in client/server mode, using TCP/IP.

A socket is a communication connection that appears to be much like a file in a Perl program. The Perl program can write to and read from sockets. Sockets originated with the University of California at Berkeley version of UNIX. They are supported by the Perl `Socket` module.

The first step in building either a client or a server is to create a socket, which is done with a call to the `socket` function, that is part of the `Socket` module. The `socket` function takes four parameters, the first of which is a socket filehandle. It serves the same purpose as a filehandle for a file: It is the program's name for the socket. The second parameter indicates the protocol, which for us will always be an Internet socket. This is specified with the `PF_INET` constant, defined in the `Socket` module. The third parameter indicates the socket type, which for us will always be TCP. This is specified with the `SOCK_STREAM` constant, defined in the `Socket` module. The last parameter indicates the number of the protocol on your system, which is obtained by calling a function in `Socket`, `getprotobyname`, using as a parameter `"tcp"`. Because `socket` returns false if it fails, calls to `socket` are often used with `die`. So, to create a socket that uses TCP/IP, the following code can be used:

```
use Socket;
$proto = getprotobyname("tcp");
socket(MY_SOCKET, PF_INET, SOCK_STREAM, $proto) ||
  die "Could not create socket $!";
```

We now describe the process of constructing a socket-based server. The first step is to connect the socket created earlier to a network address, using the `bind` function. Before describing `bind`, however, we must discuss the computation of one of its parameters, the Internet address of potential clients. This is built from the chosen port number, the address type, and the Internet address of the client. The simplest server is allowed to connect to any client, for which there is a constant defined in `Socket`, `INADDR_ANY`, which combines the address type for the Internet and the code for "any client." This is in turn combined with the port number with `sockaddr_in`, as in

```
sockaddr_in($port, INADDR_ANY);
```

It is common to use this call as the second parameter to `bind`. Like `socket`, `bind` returns false if it fails, so it is usually used with `die`. For example, consider the following code:

```
bind(MY_SOCKET, sockaddr_in($port, INADDR_ANY)) ||
    die "Could not bind socket $!";
```

Next, we call the `listen` function to have the program pay attention to the port "watching" for incoming connections. Like many of the other functions in `Socket`, the `listen` function returns false if it fails, so we call it with `die`. An example call to `listen` is

```
listen(MY_SOCKET, 1) || die "Could not listen $!";
```

The second parameter to `listen` is the size of the waiting queue for processes attempting to send messages to the port. For our simple example, `1` will suffice.

The last step in building the server is to construct a loop that includes a call to the `accept` function, which accepts incoming messages. The second parameter to `accept` is the socket filehandle of the server. The first parameter is the socket filehandle of the client, which is created when the message arrives. Every incoming message causes the creation of a new client socket. The `fork` function is often used to create a new child process for each incoming message, but because we chose not to describe `fork` in Section 10.3, we will not do that in our example. When the message has been processed, the client socket is closed.

Input from the client socket can be read with the line input operator, using the client socket filehandle. A message can be sent back to the client from the server, using `print` with the client socket filehandle as its first parameter.

For illustration purposes, this program sets up a server that simply sends a greeting message to any client that communicates with it. We use the number 1234 for the port number, assuming it is available. On UNIX systems, the first 1024 port numbers are reserved for the operating system. The program is as follows:

```
# sserver.pl - a server socket that just returns a greeting

use Socket;

# Select a port number (any number > 1024)

$port = 1234;

# Get the proto and create a socket

$proto = getprotobyname("tcp");
socket(MY_SOCKET, PF_INET, SOCK_STREAM, $proto) ||
    die "Could not create socket $!";

# Bind the socket to "any" client

bind(MY_SOCKET, sockaddr_in($port, INADDR_ANY)) ||
    die "Could not bind socket $!";

# Listen for messages & display a message stating that it is

listen(MY_SOCKET, 1) || die "Could not listen $!";
print "Server listening on port $port \n";

# Loop to accept and "handle" messages from clients

while ($paddr = accept(CLIENT, MY_SOCKET)) {
    print CLIENT "Greetings from your server \n";
}

close(CLIENT);
```

We now discuss how a simple client is constructed to communicate with our server. Once again, we must create a socket. This code is exactly as that in the server. Next, we must build the Internet address of the host. The host name can be input to the client program as a command line argument. With the host name, we build the Internet address of the host using two functions: `inet_aton` and `sockaddr_in`. The `inet_aton` function takes the host name as its parameter and returns the Internet address of the host. The sockaddr_in function combines the Internet address from inet_aton with the port number to get a value to which the client can connect. The program is as follows:

```perl
# sclient.pl - a client for sserver.pl
# The host name must be provided on the command line
use Socket;

# Select a port number (just a number > 1024)

$port = 1234;

# Get proto and create the socket

$proto = getprotobyname("tcp");
socket(MY_SOCKET, PF_INET, SOCK_STREAM, $proto) ||
    die "Could not create socket $!";

# Get the host name from the command line

if ($#ARGV >= 0) {
    $host = $ARGV[0];
}
else {
    die "Error - no host provided on command line $!";
}

# Build the network address of the server

$iaddr = inet_aton($host);
$paddr = sockaddr_in($port, $iaddr);

# Connect to the server

connect(MY_SOCKET, $paddr) || die "Could not connect $!";

# Simply print the message received from the server

while ($data = <MY_SOCKET>) {
    print "$data \n";
}

close (MY_SOCKET);
```

10.5 USING UNIX DBM DATABASES

Most versions of UNIX include a simple database management system for dealing with lightweight database applications. This system is supported by the Data Base Management (DBM) library of functions, which are easy to use and accessible in Perl programs.

Perl version 5 introduced a new way of accessing databases by using the tie and untie functions. Because of the complexity of these functions and the intended brevity of this book, we describe the original approaches to database usage, rather than `tie/untie`.

The structure of a DBM database is a list of key/value pairs. Because this is the same structure as that of a hash, a DBM database is used in Perl by connecting the database to a hash. All stores to the hash are mirrored onto the database. A program that accesses a previously built database connects that database to a hash and accesses the hash. A DBM database is actually stored as two files, one whose name has the `.dir` extension and one whose name has the `.pag` extension. The `.dir` file is an index into the `.pag` file, where the data is stored.

One of the most common uses of DBM in Perl programs is to provide persistent hashes; that is, a hash storage structure that persists between runs of the program or collection of programs that use it.

The function `dbmopen` is used to both create new DBM databases and to open existing DBM databases. Its first parameter is the name of the hash. The second is the name of the database, which is actually the nonextended name of the two files that store the database. The third parameter is the UNIX access mode for the database, which has the same meaning as the access mode for files and directories. For example, to create a new DBM database to store employee names and their salaries, which are to be stored in the program in the `%salaries` hash, we could use

```perl
dbmopen(%salaries, salary_db, 0666) ||
    die "Could not open salary_db $!";
```

The two files this creates are named `salary_db.dir` and `salary_db.pag`. If there are any values in `%salaries` when `dbmopen` is called, they will not be put in the database. Therefore, you must connect the hash to the database before putting anything in the hash. After connecting the hash to the database, anything you do to the hash happens to the database, specifically adding, changing, and deleting elements.

To connect a hash to an existing database, the special mode parameter `undef` must be used. Otherwise, `dbmopen` will create a new database, destroying any existing database with the same name.

When your Perl program is finished accessing a DBM database, it should close it (breaking the connection between the program hash and the database files), using `dbmclose`, which takes as its one parameter the name of the hash, *not* the database.

Suppose that we have an existing `salaries` database and need to update it with new information from the keyboard. The following program will accomplish this:

```perl
# update.pl
#  Input: A list of names and salaries from the keyboard
# Output: The input used to update the salary_db database

# Connect the database to the hash

dbmopen(%salaries, salary_db, 0666) ||
    die "Could not open salary_db $!";

# Read the keyboard data and update the database

print "Please type an employee name: ";

while ($name = <STDIN>) {
```

```
        chomp $name;
        print "Please type the new salary: ";
        $salaries{$name} = <STDIN>;
        print "Please type an employee name: ";
}

dbmclose(%salaries);
```

If a listing of a database is needed, you could use

```
        foreach $name (keys %salaries) {
            print "The salary of $name is: $salaries{$name} \n";
        }
```

However, this is a rather slow way to create the listing, because it requires reading the disk file twice (once to get the keys and once to get the values for the keys). Using each to get the elements requires just one pass over the file, as in

```
        while (($name, $salary) = each(%salaries)) {
            print "The salary of $name is: $salary \n";
        }
```

10.6 GRAPHICAL USER INTERFACES USING TK

Tk is a graphical user interface (GUI) facility associated with the scripting language, tcl. Because of the simplicity and power of Tk, a module, Tk.pm, has been built to provide some of the capabilities of Tk to Perl programs. Tk.pm is often referred to as Perl/Tk. Perl/Tk provides the usual GUI widgets, such as buttons, checkbuttons, radiobuttons, menus, and scrollbars. As with other topics in this chapter, we will discuss only a few of the features of Perl/Tk.

Perl/Tk is not part of the standard Perl distribution, but is easily obtainable from CPAN. Best of all, like other Perl modules, it is free. As was the case with CGI.pm in Chapter 9, Tk.pm is an object-oriented module, but this time we will use it as such.[3] Specifically, we will call functions through objects by using the arrow operator.

The first step in building a Perl/Tk GUI is to create a main window, into which all the program's widgets will appear. This window object is created with new on MainWindow, which returns a reference to the new MainWindow object, as in

```
        $big_window = new MainWindow;
```

The main window is the parent widget of all of the widgets in a GUI. All widgets appear in the main window and are created by calls to functions through the reference ($big_window) to the $Main_window object. So, the functions to create the GUI in the main window are called with the form

```
        $big_window -> Function_Name;
```

The simplest widget is a button. Buttons provide users with switches for inputting simple information or for requests for actions to be executed by the program. A button object is created with a call to the Button function, which can take several parameters.

---

[3]Recall that in Chapter 9, we treated CGI.pm as if it were a simple collection of functions.

Parameters to the functions in Perl/Tk are usually passed in the same form as those to `CGI.pm` functions. They are specified in keyword form, with the name of the parameter appearing first, with an attached dash (-). This is followed by an implication symbol, =>, and the value of the actual parameter.

All buttons require a name or title, which is specified with the `text` parameter. If a button is to cause some program action when it is pressed, that action is described in a function called a *callback* function. The particular callback function for a button is specified with the `command` parameter. For example, consider

```
$quit_button = $big_window -> Button(-text => "Quit",
                                      -command => \&quit);
```

where `Quit` is the title and `quit` is the name of the callback function. We have now created a button widget, but it is not yet displayed on the screen. This is accomplished by calling the `pack` function on the button object, as in

```
$quit_button -> pack;
```

The `pack` function can be given a number of different parameters that allow the user to specify the placement of the widget in the main window, but we will not discuss them.

The last thing required to make the button work is to create a loop to watch the button for user actions. This is done by calling `MainLoop`. In the simple case of our `$quit_button`, we could use

```
MainLoop;
sub quit {
    exit;
}
```

All of this together appears as follows:

```
# quit.pl - A simple quit button

use Tk;

# Create the main window

$big_window = new MainWindow;

# Create and pack the quit button

$quit_button = $big_window -> Button(-text => "Quit",

                                     -command => \&quit);

$quit_button -> pack;

# Loop to watch the button

MainLoop;

# The callback function

sub quit {
    print "The quit button was pressed \n";
    exit;
}
```

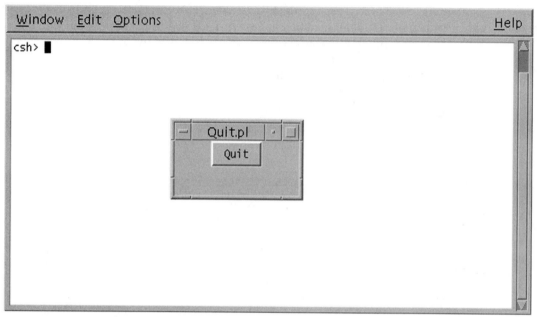

Figure 10.1 A simple quit button, using Perl/Tk

The screen created by this code is shown in Figure 10.1.

To simply place text in the main window, we use a `Label` object. The text of a `Label` object is static—it is not associated with any widget or callback function:

```
$title = $big_window -> Label(-text => "My Widget Box");
```

Recall that radio buttons are buttons in a group that are related by the characteristic that only one of them can be in the pressed state or status, at a time. If you press one and some other button is currently pressed, that button will become unpressed by your action. The value of a collection of radio buttons is stored in a program variable that you name when creating the radio buttons. The specific radio button that is pressed can be determined by examining the value of this variable. A radio button is created with a call to `Radiobutton`, which can take several parameters. The value variable is specified with the `value` parameter to `Radiobutton`. The initial value of a radio button collection is specified by assigning that value to the value variable of the radio button collection. Obviously, all of the radio buttons in a collection use the same value variable. To create a collection of buttons together, we first create a frame within the main window in which to place them. This is explained next.

Some of the possible parameters to the `Radiobutton` function are as follows:

`text`	which gives a name for the radio button.
`background`	which specifies the background color of the radio button.
`foreground`	which specifies the color to be used to display the button's name.
`variable`	which specifies the variable that stores the radio button collection's value.
`command`	which specifies the callback function for the radio button.

A frame object is created with a call to `Frame` through the window object, as in

```
$frame = $big_window -> Frame;
```

Characteristics of the frame can be set by calling the `configure` function, which can take several parameters. In the next example, we call `configure` to set the background color of the frame with the `background` parameter. We set the width of the frame's border with the `borderwidth` parameter. The border width is the distance in pixels between the frame border and its widgets.

After packing the buttons we created, we must also pack the frame.

The example that follows illustrates these ideas. It creates three buttons that can be used to change the background color of the frame.

```perl
# tstradio.pl - a program to illustrate Tk radio buttons

use Tk;

# Create the main window and the frame for the buttons

$big_window = new MainWindow;
$frame = $big_window -> Frame;
$frame -> configure(-background => "red",
                    -borderwidth => 60);

# Set the default color for the radio button collection

$color = "red";

# Create the three radio buttons, one for blue, one for red,
#   and one for green frame background color

$blue =   $frame -> Radiobutton (-text        => "Blue",
                                 -background  => "yellow",
                                 -foreground  => "blue",
                                 -variable    => \$color,
                                 -value       => "blue",
                                 -command     => \&bluebk);
$red =    $frame -> Radiobutton (-text        => "Red",
                                 -background  => "yellow",
                                 -foreground  => "red",
                                 -variable    => \$color,
                                 -value       => "red",
                                 -command     => \&redbk);
$green = $frame -> Radiobutton (-text        => "Green",
                                 -background  => "yellow",
                                 -foreground  => "green",
                                 -variable    => \$color,
                                 -value       => "green",
                                 -command     => \&greenbk);

# Create the quit button

$quit = $frame -> Button (-text => "Quit",
```

```
                          -foreground => "white",
                          -background => "purple",
                          -command    => \&quit);

# Pack the buttons and the frame

$blue -> pack;
$red -> pack;
$green -> pack;
$quit -> pack;
$frame -> pack;

# Create the loop to watch the buttons

MainLoop;

# The callback functions

sub bluebk {
    $frame -> configure(-background => "blue");
}

sub redbk {
    $frame -> configure(-background => "red");
}

sub greenbk {
    $frame -> configure(-background => "green");
}

sub quit {
    exit;
}
```

The screen generated by this code is shown in Figure 10.2.

10.7　SUMMARY

Directories can be created, deleted, and traversed in Perl. Wild-card characters can be used to specify categories or globs of files in directories.

UNIX account information can be retrieved with getpwent. Information about a system and some account information can be retrieved in Windows by using functions from the Win32 module.

Perl provides two different ways to launch other programs, backticks and the system function. These are normally used to execute programs that can be run directly from the command line.

Sockets provide a simple standard method for communicating among possibly distributed processes. Sockets and the TCP/IP protocol are the primary method for providing Internet processing. Perl's Socket module provides the software to create and use sockets. The capabilities of Socket are similar to those available in C. TCP/IP server communications are made possible by creating a socket, binding it to an Internet address,

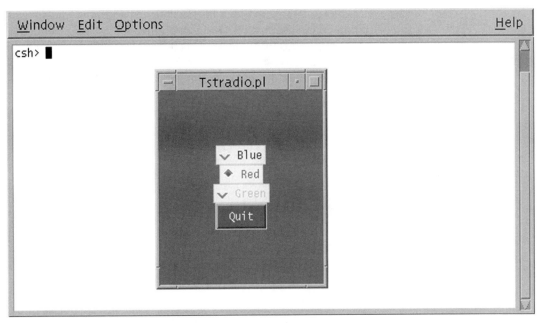

Figure 10.2   A set of radio buttons, using Perl/Tk

and then listening to the socket for messages. Clients are constructed by creating a socket and binding it to an Internet address of a server.

The UNIX simple database management system, DBM, is available to Perl programs through hashes. A hash variable in a program is connected to the database with a call to dbmopen. After such a connection is made, any manipulations to the hash are mirrored in the database. In essence, a DBM database is a persistent hash.

The graphical user interface capabilities of Tk are made available to Perl programs through the module, Tk.pm. The Tk facilities are powerful and easy to use.

10.8   EXERCISES

1. Write a Perl program for the following specification:

    Input: The name of a directory and a file name extension, both from the command line.

    Output: All files in the given directory with the given name extension that are more than 1,000 bytes long.

2. (For UNIX users only) Write a Perl program that displays the names of all users whose accounts begin with a letter between 'a' and 'g' and do not include any digits.

3. (For UNIX users only) Put the sserver.pl and sclient.pl programs on two different UNIX machines and test them.

4.   Write a Perl program that makes additions to and deletions from a DBM file containing names and social security numbers, both represented as strings. The input to this program is an even-length list of lines, where the first line has a name, the second has a social security number of the person named in the first line, and so forth. If a name is followed by a 0 social security number, the name is to be deleted from the file; otherwise it is added.

5.   Modify the radio button program in Section 10.6 (`tstradio.pl`) to use a menu instead of the radio buttons to select the background color. Provide menu entries for at least four different colors.

Index